"RABBI BEN KAMIN is a compassionate expert on spiritual inclusiveness, especially as it applies to a generation of deeply feeling yet religiously disenchanted younger people. In this refreshingly accessible guide for those seeking a place to alight, he builds a bridge between ironclad traditions and newer demographics that require flexibility. His enlightened application of 'spiritual pragmatism' liberates biblical characters from theological traps and makes them as real, flawed, and human as we are."

ERIC FINGERHUT
Former US Congressman
President of Hillel International

"To BEN KAMIN, God is not a distant rule-giver, but a creator who continues, eon after eon and day after day, to interact with humans. This book, with its lyrical prose, invites readers to connect the stories of the Bible with their own realities of today in a way few clergy have done before. Far from asking spiritual seekers to abandon the Bible or their religion's approach to it, Rabbi Ben invites readers to consider the human realities beneath the sometimes contradictory biblical stories. The book is a wonder of reasoning tempered with love, of historical fact tempered with modern realities. For those on a spiritual path, I cannot recommend it highly enough."

LAURA HARRISON MCBRIDE
Publisher, Muffin Dog Press, author, and award-winning journalist

"AN EXTREMELY TIMELY and insightful book written for the many people who are dissatisfied with religion but want more than strict secularism.

Millennials are looking for meaning, an older population is rejecting materialism, conscious capitalism is ascending, and Pope Francis is more and more appealing as a world religious leader. Rabbi Ben Kamin has captured the old-time spiritual values hidden in scripture. This is a must-read for everyone, regardless of faith background."

JOSEPH W. JORDAN
Consultant, speaker, and author of the
best-selling book Living a Life of Significance

"RABBI BEN KAMIN'S new book is filled with hope and tolerance and a unique understanding of the original intentions of the Bible. As a survivor of four Nazi death camps, I can attest to what happens when people completely judge and humiliate others just because we have a different view, a different background, or a different understanding of God. Kamin's book is the inspirational opposite of racism and separatism. In speaking to people around the world about religious bigotry, I have found that so many are afflicted with the need to make themselves bigger by making others smaller. Rabbi Kamin reminds us that in the eyes of God, we are all the same size and we all have equal value."

LOU DUNST
Holocaust survivor and inspirational speaker

"THIS IS A BOOK for all those who have voted with their feet and walked away from organized religion, yet, at the same time, have a spiritual yearning to deeply connect with what is holy and sacred in the world and make meaning of their lives."

RABBI KERRY M. OLITZKY
Executive Director, Big Tent Judaism
Author of Life's Daily Blessings *and*
The Rituals & Practices of a Jewish Life

"IN A WORLD WHERE anything is possible and everything is uncertain, Ben Kamin embraces the doubts we all have about religion and emerges with faith in human attributes that reflect divinity no matter what one's path to God. *I Don't Know What to Believe* is a superb book for anyone fed up with theologies that divide and thrive on fear. Kamin takes a deep dive into the Bible and demonstrates how being human is what it means to be Godly, and how no one has a monopoly on faith."

RABBI MICAH D. GREENSTEIN
Senior Rabbi, Temple Israel

"RABBI BEN KAMIN presents ancient texts with futuristic precision as through a high-powered telescope that peers into the past with a command to experience the deeper edges of life within and in front of humanity. A great, mesmerizing storyteller, Kamin brings the mystery of faith doctrines into the reaches of contemporary contemplation and discovery. He audaciously invites 'believers' to argue with God and demand justice, liberation, and salvation for every human person. Personal, cultural, and global in scope, *I Don't Know What to Believe* incites our appetite to explore the essence of life and find God within the sacred existence of every human person."

REV. DR. ART CRIBBS
Executive Director, Interfaith Movement for Human Integrity
Administrative Pastor, Los Angeles Filipino-American
United Church of Christ

I DON'T KNOW WHAT TO BELIEVE

I Don't Know What to
BELIEVE

MAKING SPIRITUAL PEACE
WITH YOUR RELIGION

Ben Kamin

CRP®

CENTRAL RECOVERY PRESS

Las Vegas

Central Recovery Press (CRP) is committed to publishing exceptional materials addressing addiction treatment, recovery, and behavioral healthcare topics.

For more information, visit www.centralrecoverypress.com.

Publisher: Central Recovery Press
3321 N. Buffalo Drive
Las Vegas, NV 89129

21 20 19 18 17 16   1 2 3 4 5

Library of Congress Cataloging-in-Publication Data
Names: Kamin, Ben.
Title: I don't know what to believe: making spiritual peace with your religion / Ben Kamin.
Description: Las Vegas : Central Recovery Press, 2016.
Identifiers: LCCN 2015040821 | ISBN 9781942094043 (pbk. : alk. paper)
Subjects: LCSH: Spirituality.
Classification: LCC BL624 .K33155 2016 | DDC 204--dc23
LC record available at http://lccn.loc.gov/2015040821

Author photo taken by Photos by Solange in San Diego, CA. Used with permission.

Publisher's Note: This book contains general information about spirituality and religious traditions. Central Recovery Press books represent the experiences and opinions of their authors only. Every effort has been made to ensure that events, institutions, and statistics presented in our books as facts are accurate and up-to-date. To protect their privacy, the names of some of the people and institutions in this book may have been changed.

Cover design and interior by Marisa Jackson

TO THE MEMORY OF
MARTIN LUTHER KING, JR.

*"We must learn that to
expect God to do everything
while we do nothing
is not faith but superstition."*

TABLE OF CONTENTS

INTRODUCTION

THIS BOOK IS WRITTEN to offer answers, direction, and validation to the many thoughtful people who feel excluded or judged because they prefer a spiritual life over what the organized religions are offering. I am a longtime rabbi, a product of institutional faith and structured liturgies. Some time ago, I came to the conviction that the church/synagogue/mosque system has essentially failed to motivate or repair the world. I realized that a critical, imaginative look at scripture actually reveals that God does not play favorites and neither should we.

In 2013, a landmark report issued by the Pew Research Center declared that Americans are more "un-churched" and less affiliated with institutions of organized religion than at any time. This was the latest charted indication of the trend toward disenfranchisement, especially among younger people, from theological centers and ideas. At the same time, all the denominations report a precipitous rise in intermarriage (over 60 percent in the Jewish community) and blended families, further diluting cultural and doctrinal differences or adding different characteristics. That same year, the *New York Times* reported a 45 percent interdenominational intermarriage rate among Christians (to other Christian faith sect members or to Jews and Muslims), as well as the "relatively high rates of intermarriage of American Muslims."

The regulated religious agencies feel threatened even as there is a striking decline in people seeking to become priests, ministers, imams, and rabbis. The Catholic Church, for example, is so short-handed that recruitment literature for priestly careers is regularly found in pews and, all-too-often, untrained deacons or lay volunteers are substituting for professionally educated and trained clergy in the church and other denominations. This is creating a further disconnect, in terms of trust and performance, between members and clerics in churches, temples, and mosques. In the latter culture, sharia judges and professors are often being recruited to fill in for missing imams.

At the same time, previously rigid barriers are being broken in our society, notably in the recognition of women as clergy and, particularly, the legalization of same-sex marriage and the ordination of openly gay clergy people. This has created a deep polarization between socially conservative and liberal elements of our nation, triggering a strong backlash of superciliousness on the part of those on the right when it comes to issues such as abortion rights, prayer in schools, and whether or not this is "a Christian country."

Those on the liberal side of the spectrum often feel ambivalent, rebellious, or just left out. They don't want others to tell them they are "damned" if they do or don't do this or that. They don't want to have their parents' faith tradition prevent them from marrying whomever they wish to marry—regardless of religion or heritage. They are disillusioned by what they feel is the increasingly sectarian nature of politics. They resent the arrogance of rabbis who marginalize women liturgically and demean Jewish denominations that are not "Torah-true"; they are weary of Christian fundamentalists; and they are wary of the evangelists. They are understandably frightened of Islamic terrorism, but don't wish to fall into the facile route of stereotyping Muslims. They want inclusiveness and tolerance and they are turning to mysticism, ranging from the creation of post-denominational prayer centers to meditation and yoga practice to Eastern worship ideology and/or community service in place of routinized ritual and obeisance. Even those who identify as atheists want to feel connected to something.

It is my position, after over thirty-five years in the rabbinate and in social services, that what these people want is normal. They want answers about the mysteries of human life that are not canned or even discriminatory; they want a God that doesn't judge people but for the goodness of their souls. They want to find some kindness and consolation in scriptural texts. They look at the legacy of religiously driven global war and at the financial, ethical, and sexual scandals that are rampant in organized religion, and they want something more hopeful, more tolerant, and more healing for themselves and for their children.

They need a scrupulous, honest guide to spirituality that respects the traditions but does not regard them as necessarily binding or inviolate in their lives. They want guidance in order to share their spiritual yearnings with others that make some sense against the sectarian chaos and conflict that prevails in this country. They want gentle rituals that flow within nature and that they can actually understand. They don't want to live in a world of "all good" or "all evil" because they are sophisticated and recognize that life is nuanced. They want sensible answers, and they don't want to feel guilty because they have questions, such as:

- ❖ Why does my parents' religion have to define me?
- ❖ If I don't baptize my child or don't send him or her to Hebrew School, will he or she be damned to eternal punishment?
- ❖ Am I God's child even if I don't go to religious services?

- ❖ Doesn't scripture include me in its ideology regardless of how much scripture I have learned or know?
- ❖ Are all the characters in scripture saints or perfect role models?
- ❖ How do I follow my own spirituality while still respecting my parents' traditions?

One reason I know organized religion has generally failed is because it is declaring this failure itself by diverting attention from its dogmas via social gatherings, retreats, initial complimentary memberships, free food, religious rock music festivals, and a variety of other improvisations. Despite the efforts and energy invested in these venues churches and synagogues are merging or closing down, clergy are retiring early and not being replaced, and budgets are being slashed. Only the fundamentalists and zealots, the ones who maintain that it's their way to heaven or you are going to hell, well, only they survive and dig in.

This book is not concerned with the future of churches or temples or synagogues or mosques. This book is concerned with the people out there, decent, hardworking, caring folks who want to be included in a life enriched with spiritual meaning and devoid of judgment. My hope is that they will benefit from an established religious leader telling them why and how they are as much God's children as anybody else.

The text is not our homeland; life is. God is not to be determined; God is to be discovered—like dawn is a personal experience and the moon is seen in as many ways as there are eyes that can look up.

I have written this book after decades in the pulpit life, in one form or another, and this book is not an argument with tradition. It is an argument for transcendence. My own faith community long ago established that God created the world, but people are creating it. Not Jews—people. We human beings are God's partners. We invented these religions, not God. The Bible starts out with absolutely no reference to creeds.

The creation story begins in a garden and the name of the first man, Adam, means "humanity." Then Adam and his mate Eve departed the garden because they had painfully learned wisdom and awareness. Some say they were banished—much too harsh and inconsistent with the kindness of heaven, the tenderness of Jesus, or the best liturgies of any mosque or pagoda. They left because it was time for them to grow and to find a way to balance belief with reality.

This book will present several categories of belief and action that don't belong to anybody but you. These range from the meaning of creation to the question of how to live with the Bible to what all the faiths absolutely agree upon when it comes to defining a good person. This book is not going to stop the insanity of jihad, the insensitivity of rabbinic cabals, or the extremism of Christian evangelism. It's not going to prevent Hindus and Muslims from killing each other in India or Muslims from exterminating Coptic Christians in Egypt. This book will not bring peace to the city of Jerusalem.

This book, however, using a philosophy I call "spiritual pragmatism," will show you how to believe in what you choose to believe and not feel tainted, condemned, or excluded. Spiritual pragmatism means knowing religion works best when it doesn't tell you what to think, but rather to think. Nobody in the Bible who is considered a heroic figure got that way without thinking, questioning, and even doubting.

Like you and me, these men and women didn't simply comply. They came to conclusions after life threw them some real challenges. Some days they felt good about God; other days not so much. They didn't always know what to believe. They relied on their instincts and none of them ever held a prayer book in their hands. They did the best they could, and we acquire insight from their stories exactly because, as we shall see, each and every one of them had flaws, committed offenses, and grappled with family dysfunctions. Jesus wrestled with temptation; Moses had anger-management issues; and Mohammed betrayed a prejudice against the blind. Sarah dreamed of becoming a mother and put up with an insensitive husband. Rebekah was a deceiver, and Mary Magdalene was a seductress possessed by demons.

These people are interesting because they were hardly perfect. We learn the most from them when we realize they were real people—parents, children, spouses, friends, enemies, neighbors, and coworkers—just like you and me. The struggle to make peace with your religion is as old as the Bible and as new as today's newspaper.

Chapter One

FIRST PLANT THE TREE

THE HOT BREEZE WAS blowing across the rocky terrain south of Jerusalem, bending the nearby olive trees and sending dust upward toward the purple sky. The farmer knelt carefully over the slight hole he had just dug in the stubborn earth with a wooden spade, a small pail of water set down to his right. His hands were firm and covered with soil, a mixture of sand and gravel and clay that caked on his dark palms and looked pink in the afternoon light.

He thought he heard the wail of a ram's horn coming from the walled city in the distance but focused instead on the fragile green sapling he had laid down on the ground a few moments before. He was almost prayer-like, keenly aware of the sapling's vulnerability, its need for moisture and tenderness, its longing to be set into the ground and drink in the rare rain and then, in time, give shade to someone. The man hummed something to himself—a wordless melody that was old and unidentifiable and yet as familiar to him as the wind.

There was nothing else happening in the world for this grizzled farmer, his brownish head protected under a smudged woven cloth *keffiyeh*, the headdress held tight with a string cord, shielding him from the sun as his long and crusted fingers pulled away heaps of dirt. He was well-acquainted with the yellow-gray silts and sediments of the Judean basin and could even sense the invisible, microscopic organisms living within the soil he carefully shaped into planting sod for his young tree. The ram's horn sounded again. People being called to worship or some new proclamation.

"Do it this way or you are damned."

"Listen to me or you are out."

The city was so often in some kind of uproar, he thought. *I have important work to do.*

He did not hear the voice of the other man at first. His mind, hands, back, and brain were all one motion of devotion and resolve. He wanted to plant the tree.

"Man!" The other fellow stood over him and cried out. "What are you doing there? You need to come to Jerusalem with me right now. Why would you tally here?"

The farmer was reluctantly pulled out of his trance of work and dedication. He looked up and blinked into the bright light, barely able to see the face of the excited intruder.

"Why do I have to come with you to Jerusalem?"

"Why? Haven't you heard? The Messiah has arrived!"

"I see. But I am planting this sapling right now."

The visitor took a step closer. His body momentarily blocked the sun and the farmer could see his face and his eyes and what he saw was a good man looking for hope in a bleak world. He saw that loneliness, that yearning to belong to something, to fit in somewhere, to believe in some great power that could turn everything into easy answers.

My visitor does not know the peace of the fields and the wisdom of the skies, he thought. *He is not running to Jerusalem because the ram's horn is blowing. He is running to find himself because his soul is empty and hurting.*

"I understand what you are telling me, my friend," said the farmer, setting his spade down and slowly standing up. "I have respect. But we have two positions here. You want to go to see a Messiah you don't know anything about. I want to plant a tree I know everything about."

"What shall we do?" asked the visitor, his eyes growing a little wild from the predicament presented so calmly by the old man who was digging a hole in the desert.

"Well, there's a rabbi nearby," said the farmer. "His tent is just beyond this olive grove. Let's go ask him what he thinks about our problem. I agree ahead of time to abide by his decision about what you and I should do."

The other man nodded and they walked together to visit the sage.

The rabbi greeted them and gave them both some water to drink. The three of them sat down in the tent, which was cool and pleasant.

"Rabbi," began the farmer, "this man tells me I must run with him to Jerusalem immediately. Because of the ram's horn."

"Why would you not accompany him?" inquired the rabbi.

The other man interrupted: "He won't come to see the Messiah! They say the Messiah has arrived. He'd rather finish planting this one little tree in the middle of nowhere. Can you believe it?"

"Believe what, my son?" asked the rabbi. "That the Messiah is waiting in Jerusalem or that this farmer wants to plant his tree?" The rabbi was weary and kind all at once. He had seen and heard a lot of things in his life but seemed quite content in his tent.

"I am confused by your question, Rabbi," said the man in a hurry to reach the city.

"Then you are beginning to stop and think, my son. That is good."

The farmer was thinking about his sapling, laying and baking on the hot earth, still unplanted. He spoke: "Rabbi, I have pledged to my friend that I will abide by your judgment on this situation. Perhaps you can direct us."

The rabbi smiled as he sat and thought for a moment. Then he considered his two visitors with a serene look. There was a twinkle in his eye. He leaned a bit toward the farmer and said, "First plant the tree. It's more of a sure thing."

THIS STORY IS TAKEN from an old rabbinic parable and it speaks to the purpose of this book. The early devotions and aspirations of the world's three major organized religions convey stories and ideas that completely refute the terrifying trend of extremism, violence, and terrorism committed in the name of these traditions. Not one of these traditions was meant to turn its followers into cult members nor have their disciples morph into the slaves of self-proclaimed, often brutal "deliverers."

This cautionary notice appears in the early Bible: "If a prophet (the term here used as a warning) or a dreamer of dreams arises among you, and if he says, 'Let us go after other gods,' which you have not known, 'and let us serve them,' you shall not listen to the words of that prophet or that dreamer of dreams."

At its core, religion is not supposed to tell you what to think; it's supposed to tell you to think. Within a hundred years of the origin of the sapling story presented above, Jesus pointed to a mulberry tree and challenged his apostles to think of the tree's grace and power and use the tree as a metaphor for faith. Seven centuries later, Mohammed declared: "If a Muslim plants a seedling or cultivates a field, whenever a bird a human or an animal eats of it, it will be counted as a charity for him." He is also quoted in Islamic verses as admonishing a fellow cleric who made a bigoted remark while they attended the funeral of a Jew. The Prophet replied, "Was he not a human being?"

The big religions—which loved the Earth, pleaded for social justice, and upheld personal freedom, and, yes, applauded love—appear to have been co-opted by fundamentalists and zealots. Hate crowds the pages of theological manuals, excommunication notices, and *fatwās*. This is not just recently; the path of religion is drenched with blood and littered with bones. Like a bad dream, we seem to be reliving its most melancholy and medieval travesties; we are living in a world of televised crusades and theological wars. It leaves us sitting in all-but-empty churches listening to useless pieties and waiting in choking, endless security lines filing past digital checkpoints. We are uncomfortable, wary, tired, and jumpy. If it's not another suicide bomber or civil war atrocity, then it's the latest scandalized bishop or charismatic preacher or disgraced rabbi. It leaves people like you and me shaking our heads and proclaiming: "I don't know what to believe!"

And what person of any intelligence, any mercy, and any humility would not be asking this question? We are hardly all atheists; we need faith and caring and some rituals to connect us to our childhood homes, our parents, and our grandparents. We see something in a lit candle—a festive hope or a remembered soul. We find relief in confession; we get comfort and pleasure from holiday meals; we like to feel we can kneel on the earth, on a rug, or on the floor of a pagoda and speak quietly with God. We just want to trust the officers of God's houses, and we want to make sense of what's become a skewed scripture.

We don't want somebody to tell us he or she is a messiah; we'd prefer to discover messianic moments by ourselves.

What of the little guy who can't keep pace with all the edicts or can't afford the membership dues or whose son or daughter falls in love with someone from "outside the faith?" All this guy wants is peace and acceptance, and he's not even dealing with cults or fanatics. He's dealing with a church or a mosque or a synagogue, and what he is getting is rejection and judgment. For God's sake, we clergy should be part of the solution, not part of the problem.

We will find a lot to believe in again when we are permitted to stop confusing faith with the saga of a few lionized male leaders. When we stop hearing the ram's horn as tyranny but as music. When we maintain respect for traditions but keep glory at arm's length. When we are smart enough to sprinkle the salt of skepticism upon the hard-won bread of life.

Spirituality is the story of thousands of everyday people going about their nonsensational lives until, when trouble or cruelty or cancer call, necessity intervenes, and they show up, line up, reach out, and sometimes even pray. And there is hope when those prayers are not crushed by the small-mindedness of church leaders who care more about their power than our piety.

"Take off your shoes," God admonishes Moses at the site of the Burning Bush. "You are standing on holy ground." What was this God actually saying? Moses was not at the Vatican. He was not at the Mosque of Omar. He was not even in Jerusalem. He was in the wilderness, in the middle of nowhere. In other words, wherever you feel God, that is holy ground; and what you feel and what you experience is real and it is what you believe.

A wise pastor of the Gospel once told me, "Religion works best as a salad. It has to have a variety of ingredients mixed together to come out good. Each one of us is an ingredient."

These days, too many people are inbred from childhood to follow extremist chief rabbis and self-righteous evangelicals and sexually deviant priests. There are imams who have lost their minds and any connections with Mohammed. The majority of Muslims, who honor the Prophet's historic message, have watched their faith become transposed in a regrettable way.

Mohammed was a complex and charismatic man who embraced all of the preceding faiths, affirmed the prophetic qualities of Moses and Jesus before him, and who stated: "Do not be people without minds of your own, saying that if others treat you well you will treat them well, and that if they do wrong you will do wrong. Instead, accustom yourselves to do good if people do well and not to do wrong if they do evil."

This is the beacon in whose name mothers send their children to be suicide bombers? Moses is the freedom marcher and teacher in whose standard clerics in Jerusalem spit at teenage girls, who excommunicate one another, and yearn for the destruction of the Dome of the Rock. Jesus asked, "What business is it of mine to judge those outside the church?" What are you to believe? One thing worth knowing is that the religions have somewhat fossilized into archaic, even dangerous organisms, spewing out hate and division, enslaving minds, and that you have to go back to the beginnings to rediscover that each one of us is God's equal child and all we have to believe in is pastoral kindness.

Just because some of God's professionals and profiteers have lost contact with the rhapsody, the aspirations, and the aches that came with their faiths does not mean that any one of us is going to give away our desire to believe in something or to feel a moment of awe without a priestly tutorial. In the end, the Bible is a library of ideas and people and oracles and phonies and miracles and romances and murders and music, and like the human experience itself, it is loaded with contradictions.

The Bible is, at once, the most widely published and completely unknown volume in the history of this planet. It sits unopened, like a perfunctory slab, in most every hotel room drawer on the globe. People open and shut the drawer, notice the book, but rarely pick it up. It seems to us like it belongs there—we expect it there, like some ominous reminder of forced, past devotionals or hand wringing on the part of a parent or a priest. But we rarely open or refer to it. It remains a bound mystery that we never really understood and we go on with our business.

The Jews say, "If you only have Torah, then you don't even have Torah." In other words, there's more—a lot more—to living life and believing in something than just arbitrarily quoting from one segment, or even a single passage, from a book. It's not holy because God wrote it. It's holy because men and women *inspired* by God wrote it. With each successive writer came a new layer of insight, of pain, of yearning, and breakthrough. If we surrender the authorship to God, then we human beings are just vessels and poetry dissolves into the earth.

We upgrade or discard our cellular phones within months of each edition. Our cars become outdated within minutes of leaving the dealership, but we still believe in the automobile. Does all this make a cell phone or a vehicle any less essential to us in the twenty-first century? Can't we be just as nimble with the data and the information we cherish and still pray while acknowledging that that book was canonized when people rode on camels and the only upgrade available back then was their imagination?

We know George Washington did not chop down a cherry tree. Does that make what he had to say and how he fathered the United States any less sacred? So does it really matter if Moses actually climbed up Mt. Sinai and came down forty days later with two stones inscribed, "with God's finger," and called them "the Ten Commandments?" Doesn't it matter more that we have the legacy of law and decency and the notion of honoring our parents and the prohibition against stealing from others?

As I mentioned previously, the text is not our homeland; life is. God is not to be determined; God is to be discovered—like dawn is a personal experience and the moon is seen in as many ways as there are eyes that can look up.

I remember gazing into the wedding canopy where my younger daughter exchanged marriage vows with her betrothed just a few years ago. The evening ceremony took place outdoors in an orchard-filled community complex not far inland in central Israel.

The open field, the fragrant citrus, the celestial ceiling, the bittersweet sentiments of life and generations all converted the setting into a natural sanctuary. There was a palpable holiness in the air, none of it organized, legislated, or tethered to any one creed. Muslims, Jews, and Christians, agnostics, atheists, doubters, and zealots became one in the liturgy of love and the religion of romance.

I was there, simply as the father of the bride. Ironically, even though I am a veteran rabbi, I could not perform her ceremony. Israel forbids non-Orthodox rabbis from officiating at milestone events because the fundamentalist rabbis control all such things. And they actively prevent all other inclusive denominations from functioning. The ordination of Reform and Conservative rabbis is not recognized by the government, presenting yet another travesty of organized religion and its duplicity with cynical political operatives.

But it didn't matter that night. God knew what was in my heart and my daughter knows how much I love her—therein is the sanctity. She was happy; she was no longer a child and the twigs bent under her feet toward eternity. I wasn't concerned about religious ordinances and church hypocrisies. I looked up at the glittering sky and felt the moon knew everything that had to be known.

These are the moments when you just know there is a God and the best part is you don't have to struggle with what that even means. You float in those rare interludes of tender human milestones and you cross, with some of the mystics, over the "bridge of judgment" into paradise.

You dance with the Hopi Indians, cotton strands in your hands, making flowers to symbolize the heavens. Your eyes sting with the Buddhist wisdom that those who live in these moments may yet bless this realm again with angelic insight.

You are at one with everything and your pockets—like the white burial shrouds of the Jews—are empty. Your soul is full and you are not afraid of the future. The happiness of a child is the bridge that binds this side to the other, and there you are and you comprehend for a fleeting, delicious moment why it is good to be born and it is okay to die.

I don't need anybody to tell me who or what God is and I'm not in terror over death anymore. Experience and birth and sacred promises and exceptional pain have all filled me with quiet compliance. Who can be free near a child's rapture and not know there is a God?

First plant the tree; it's more of sure thing. And it's what the true God wants us to do.

Chapter Two

MAKING SENSE OF SCRIPTURE, SAINTS, AND SAVIORS

PEOPLE ASK: "Do I have to believe the Bible was written by God to be considered a 'good' person?" That's like saying you have to borrow every book out of a library to prove that you love the library. Or asserting that scientists, who have done a great job over the centuries explaining what goes on in the universe, are all sinners and doomed to the netherworld.

The Bible was not written by God, but by men and women inspired by God. If you start with this rational view of the Bible, it will give you, here and there, a lot of meaningful insights and moral direction. And you won't get stuck on some of its significant inconsistencies in terms of narratives, ideas, and chronology.

I have been touched by the compassionate examples of many people—nurses, musicians, fire fighters, schoolteachers, hospice workers—who didn't know a lot of Bible yet exhibited a kind of goodness and dedication that was as biblical as it was unpretentious. I have also visited clergymen and temple presidents serving time in prison for corruption, embezzlement, and sexual criminality.

The Bible is an archive of disparate books, written at different times and by different authors living in different times and circumstances.

When we let other people determine what we should take out of it, then we have made the librarians into priests and we have ceased to be learners. We have choked the creativity of this literature, muffled its poetry, and stifled its many daring stories of dissent, controversy, and even spiritual ambivalence.

We have taken ourselves out of the discussion and handed it over to a few ecclesiastics, many of whom don't feel safe with it unless they are pounding you with the miracles and cataclysms that are colorful and safe and give these clerics dangerous power. What about the love stories, the sexual sonnets, the political cunnings, the family dysfunctions, the deep deceits, and pounding griefs? They are much more in tune with you and me and our little lives. You and I are less likely to witness a sea being parted than we are to win the lottery. The big marvels in some parts of scripture are diverting but they don't deliver when it comes to managing our marriages, our kids, our employers, our money problems, or our health.

The Bible is only as alive as your take on it and you are invited to grapple with it, just as you are included in its complicated tapestry of life and death, triumph and trouble. Finding this section of it repugnant and that section of it rhapsodic is actually its purpose. Believing that it is an indisputable testimony is like asserting that life is completely predictable. You've been around long enough to know that's not the case. It reduces the spiritual power of this long literature into a lunch menu and it trivializes our need to think, react, and argue with fate.

A lot of GIs carried bibles into World War II but, in the end, we beat the fascists and saved the free world with gasoline, guts, and a bit of luck. The bibles often gave our soldiers comfort, especially when they saw their friends being killed or they themselves were wounded and maimed. In the end, the Nazis didn't surrender to our gods; they succumbed to our strategy and courage.

I worry when somebody tells me the Bible is infallible and that people who don't understand this are not included in "God's plan." Without curiosity or contention, the brain becomes a rusty tool. The heart falls into a pattern of hollowness. Every one of the big faiths asserts, in one way or another, that we are God's partners. So why devolve into robots when the point of being a person is to discern, grow, create, and enjoy a few things before our brief time on Earth has come and gone?

I'm not surprised that many children and adults are looking for spiritual breakthroughs more than they are seeking liturgical formulas. Who wouldn't prefer a song to a libretto? A prayer book is a guide, and it has sanctity. But every faith, East and West, basically asserts that when we are born, we acquire a soul, and when we die, the soul returns to its creator. Families and circumstances imprint a theology upon children; heaven is dealing directly in souls. The birth canal is not lined with religious billboards. The cemetery, though it has religious symbols carved into markers, is dug into the neutral earth even as mortality is completely unaffected by doctrine, status, or vanities. Yes, a lot of people want God more than they desire formulas; after centuries of religious conflict and now, as they endure a twenty-first century global war by and on terrorism, they'd just like to sit by the still waters and savor the spirit.

Here's an irony: Vivid concepts of inclusion and realism lie quite openly in the old and later scrolls. These lyrical scrolls were scrawled by men and women who heard God, each in their own way and in the context of what they experienced or suffered. Some survived Egyptian bondage, others endured Babylonian exile, Roman oppression, Spanish inquisitions, and just wanted to make sense of the world. The writers included the early Christians who saw more insight in healing wounds than in hawking dietary laws. More often than not, they were responding to tyranny and making sense out of chaos. They were trying to defeat brutality with the power of ideas. These concepts are right there, in between the lines of tribalism and territoriality that sometimes skew the canonized texts.

These spiritual yearnings float above the thunder and lightning of the big miracles, the screaming mountains, the parting waters, and the ground opening up to swallow conspirators and sinners. These yearnings are still there in the morning after the smoke clears, the skies quiet down, and Earth sighs with relief. These sweet little truths are larger than liturgies; they are the products not of supremacy but of life's longing for itself.

Everybody is included in "God's plan," and there is no written contract. There is simply life and the reality that we are often hurt, lonely, insecure, and in need of someone else's friendship and love. What we don't need is judgment.

In 2013, Pope Francis, who does not fancy a lot of perks but sees magic in children, publicly wondered, "Who am I to judge?" He was referring to the love shared between homosexual human beings and he may have been inspired by something from the old scripture. Remember, the Bible is a library and it contains widely diverse views. In Leviticus it says that if a man lies with another man, they shall both be put to death. But Leviticus also archaically instructs us to bring young bullocks to a mountain and burn them in sacrifice, to the point where "the aroma pleases God's nostrils." The fundamentalists who are parsing human love aren't out in the fields lighting fires and offering calves to satisfy God.

Pope Francis is well acquainted with this stuff in Leviticus, but he likely also knows a poignant love story that is found later in the Bible: The romance involving the future messianic King David and Jonathan— the sensitive and brave son of the melancholy King Saul. These two lads shared something beautiful and undeniable: It's right there within the same books with all those antiquated statutes about bullocks, blood rites, and the banishment of lepers from the camp. David and Jonathan frolic in the fields and convey clear filial messages to one another. (It's in the Book of Samuel, a premier biblical prophet.) "Your father knows about us," David apprehensively says to Jonathan. "Wherever your soul goes, that's where I go," replies Jonathan.

Later, when Jonathan is killed in battle, David mourns with as stirring a message as any in the Psalms that he ultimately wrote and that has consoled Jews and Christians for millennia. Remembering the times they had wept together and kissed one another (it's verified in the text), David moans: "I grieve for you, Jonathan my brother; you were very dear to me. Your love for me was wonderful, more wonderful than that of women."

Who could read this and not know that a benevolent God does not discriminate between human loves?

They may not have told you in Hebrew school or during Sunday Bible-study classes, but David gets a full treatment in the scripture. He evolves from this youthful gay love affair into a mighty king and warrior who was also a shameless, even malicious womanizer. He played the harp and he played the field. He had multiple wives and concubines and, in one notorious instance, sent the husband of one of his lovers into a hopeless battle so that the poor man could be conveniently killed. He was plagued by critics and enemies, and some of his own children broke his heart in rebellion and insurgence. He was a person, albeit a prominent one. But he was a person like you and me—flawed, conflicted, driven by both demons and passions.

Why does the tradition embrace this kind of man and why does Christianity anoint him as the ancestor of Jesus? Because he was *real*— just as life is so glaringly real. The same intuitive and passionate man who wrote, "The Lord is my shepherd; I shall not want" is also the despicable old cad who has to have a young maiden brought to lie with him because he couldn't keep himself warm.

If this seems inexplicable, it is because life itself is inexplicable. It is never "all good" or "all bad." It is cancer to career to isolation to laughter. It is not the "all hell" or "all paradise" being poorly vended by the faiths today. It is nuanced, painful, lyrical, and it moves from defeat to compromise to a victory and then to a mistake and then a stroke of insight that amounts to bittersweet wisdom. I've seen such moments more often in a hospital room, in the cemetery, or under a wedding canopy than in a synagogue. I've heard people suddenly, gutturally, truly praying from their hearts more freely than when they were holding a prayer book and following a service outline.

The scripture was not written for angels; it was written for people. You can believe in it if you read between the lines and the edicts and the colorful miracles. You can believe in God, but you should not wait for God. Turn to God not to suddenly intervene and solve your problems—that's the pretext of cults or religious coercion, and it puts dangerous people in charge of your spirit. Turn to God (however you define God) for the strength and resolve to face your challenges—it's more of a sure thing. God is discovery; God is the result of your creativity and resolve. God is not some sort of divine bellhop.

Don't read the scripture as a series of perfect letters. The Bible is like fine leather; the flaws in it reveal its true texture and quality. The writers and the characters struggled with a tantalizing combination of truths and fears and myths and uncertainties, and they were trying to make sense of both the harshness of life and the certitude of death. In other words, they were like you and me—in our balancing act, we do best as spiritual pragmatists. We balance faith with the facts. When we are wrestling with something, we go to the library or to the web and find the right text— grateful these humanly created sources are accessible.

⁓

WHEN I WAS STILL a child, my father told me a story about his experiences as a soldier during Israel's War of Independence in 1948–49. My father was not even twenty years old, an infantry sergeant, who found himself one night around a campfire with three other sentries.

Immediately upon declaring its independence, the new state of Israel had been invaded by several neighboring Arab countries. A significant number of its fighters were emaciated Holocaust survivors who had somehow managed to gain access to the land. My father was one of the several thousand whose families had been born in what was the British mandate of Palestine.

The situation for Israel was decidedly grim. Its army was limited in numbers and munitions, divided among many languages, and generally inexperienced with everything but the notion of Jews succumbing to great and powerful forces.

Among the four soldiers, my father was more or less a secularist who wrote poetry in his native Hebrew about romance and freedom and the dreams of a people hoping to have a safe haven at last. He identified with Jewish history more than its prayer books; that history was now an existential crisis for him and his army pals.

The other three, also young, homesick, and fearful, included one Orthodox Jew, one survivor of several Nazi death camps, and one Christian American—a veteran of World War II who had now volunteered for this tour because of what he had seen Europe do to its Jews. The night was long and a cold wind blew in from the Samarian Mountains. The four men were charged to stay awake and watch for enemy infiltrators. They were exceedingly vulnerable and made shoddy jokes along with small chatter as they rubbed their gloved hands over the campfire. They methodically checked their weapons, worried about an ambush at any moment.

They began talking about God.

What was God's role in this terrible situation, my father asked out loud. Would God protect them and the precious little land they were attempting to defend? Was there even a God?

"What God?" The Holocaust survivor rang out with bitterness. "After what I saw in the camps, after I saw my parents murdered, people gassed, children thrown into sacks and beaten to death for sport, you think there is a God?"

There was an interlude of silence as the young men felt the cold begin to carve its way into their bone marrow. They added more wood to the struggling fire as the pious one began to softly sing psalms to himself. The three others looked at him as he hummed and formed ancient words that turned into little bursts of fog flying out of his mouth into the frigid midnight.

"What do you think?" My father asked the psalmist. "This one says there is no God while you shiver here praying to him."

"Of course there is a God," came the reply. "And in fact, God is so involved in this that really none of us will have anything to say about the outcome of this war, whether we live or die. It is up to God to decide if we are to have a Holy Land again. It's already been preordained in heaven so there's really nothing for us to worry about. We are just part of a higher purpose."

The American cleared his throat. "I tend to agree with that, I must say. And it's not like I go to church or anything. Not on any regular basis. I mean, sure, on Christmas Eve and such, but not all the time. But I do feel that God has something to do with this. After what happened in France and Italy and then in Germany, when I got there. Not just to the Jews, but also to my buddies and so many people I saw get killed or maimed. All the suffering. Maybe I'm here because after all of that I want to see some justice done. And that makes me feel that this Jewish story here, this reclaiming the land, is, well, biblical. I just want to see some evidence that God cares or something along those lines."

"Maybe you just like war," my father teased him. "Or you don't have any friends back in Utah where you came from." All of them laughed out loud, a cascade of nervous release and a fleeting sense of comfort in the shared predicament of mortality.

"It's Idaho," came the smiling rejoinder from the American. "And so what do you think about God?"

My father really did not know. He thought about it for a moment. "For some reason, when we sit here and talk about God in this situation we're in, I'm thinking about and really missing my mother's homemade honey pastry. I can practically smell the kitchen and the little cakes coming out of the oven, dripping with sweetness, and my mother smiling at us and telling us to wash our hands before having the treat. We did, of course, but then we always had to wash them again afterward because they were sticky with the honey. We licked our fingers before she made us wash our hands again."

The four sat around, wistful and worried and hoping to get back home to their kitchens, their bedrooms, their little sanctuaries where no one could do them any harm. After a while, my father suggested they vote on the question: Is there a God or not?

Whenever my father told me this story, he would pause and chuckle at this point. He liked it, I think, that he was the one who put the question to a vote. I would look into his deep brown eyes and notice his thick black curly hair and feel so thankful that he came home from that campfire so long ago.

"What was the vote?" I'd ask, even years after I knew the answer.

"The vote was 4–0. There is a God, but we'd better get more rifles."

Chapter Three

YOU ARE SUPPOSED
TO ARGUE WITH GOD

"What will the Egyptians say?"
—Moses to God

I T WAS JUST FOUR college chums going out to the movies. Granted, the offering that chilly winter night in Cincinnati was not typical fare. *The Exorcist* was a runaway blockbuster because of both its chilling storyline and because many religious authoritarians, especially in the Catholic Church, had a big problem with it. No wonder: In their minds, it sensationalized an extremely grave matter in church theology—the invasion of a human being by a satanic demon and the treacherous, sacred rite of exorcizing it from the person. For church zealots, this is serious business and hardly the appropriate material for Hollywood thrillers.

Three of my campus buddies joined me as we trekked out to see "the movie about the possessed girl whose head spins around." Everybody was talking about that supernatural horror film, and we were intrigued. It had already been named "the scariest film of all time" by *Entertainment Weekly*.

My friend Eric Downey was joining us against the wishes of his stern Catholic parents. I grew up a few doors from the Downeys on a street that literally ended at the gates of Our Mother of Sorrows Church. Eric, who was mercilessly mocked in the neighborhood for his grueling stutter, was one of nine children and his parents were active in the parish.

The Downeys were neighborly and generous and observed their faith with discreet service and good works. They wanted Eric, their middle son, to enter the priesthood. They did not want him to go see *The Exorcist*. For them, the motion picture was a celluloid sacrilege. Perhaps they were particularly sensitive about it because the screenplay was based upon a revealing, real-life incident that exposed a whispered-about church procedure.

In 1949, Catholic priests performed a series of such exorcisms upon an anonymous boy in Maryland known as "Roland Doe." The haunted boy's family was actually Lutheran; the busy priests just saw a Christian child possessed and controlled by a bloodcurdling spirit and this kind of situation was a denominational specialty of theirs.

The rituals were shrouded in controversy and mystery but regarded with absolute ecclesiastic solemnity by devout Catholics. No different from the many instances across the centuries when fundamentalist or mystical Jews have grappled with a *dybbuk*—the dreaded but believed evil spirit that enters into a living person. The *dybbuk* would cleave to the poor soul, cause wild dysfunction and schizophrenia, babble through the person's mouth and, as with other religious delusions, represent a separate and alien personality.

None of this dark folklore was on our minds as we boys romped to the cinema house. There were two shows playing and we almost made a last minute switch into *Blazing Saddles*—the Mel Brooks Western satire featuring Yiddish-speaking Indians and a drunken cowboy who punched out horses. Our rabid curiosity about child-actress Linda Blair's bulging, petrifying eyes; the deep, monstrous voice that inhabited her; the notorious, rotating head; and the intermittent, projectile green vomit she emitted all won us over.

The movie was at once, ghoulish, unsettling, clever, and cartoonish. There are good reasons why it spawned several sequels and is now a classic enshrined in the National Film Registry of the Library of Congress. Three of us four moviegoers exited the theater howling with mimicking demonic exertions and a show of bravado meant to distill our undeniable mixture of fun and fear. My dorm roommate Walter, an engineering student, kept speculating on "how the hell they made that girl's head spin like that."

"How the *hell*?" That was too much for Dennis, who lived across the hall. The three of us now completely keeled over in laughter and naughtiness. Then we realized that Eric was off to the side, crumpled on the sidewalk, looking like he was cringing in agony. Eric was not laughing. Eric was sobbing even as he cradled his midsection with his own arms.

Snapping out of our release and delirium, we ran over to our friend. Before we could even ask him what the matter was, he turned his head toward us, looking disturbingly like something out of the movie we just saw. His hands trembled, his shoulders convulsed, tears streamed down his face, and his eyes were two dark wells of panic.

"THAT COULD HAPPEN TO ME!" Eric cried out from somewhere within him that we young men could not categorize. A place that now alarmed us more than anything we had just viewed on screen.

"Don't you see?" He bowed his head down and wept like a fearful child. "That could happen to me. At any time. I could be possessed by a demon!"

He meant it. We understood he was not feigning anything. What was a horror flick for the other three of us was a grim and shocking liturgical reality for our buddy. And this was, at least for me, a marker on my relationship with religion—even as I was planning a career in religion.

Eric eventually recovered from his trauma. In a way, the shrill alarm he experienced served to cleanse his sectarian-sullied soul of the indoctrinations, the propaganda, and the superstitions. I was close enough to him to learn that two of the parish priests, certainly at their own professional peril, defying the rectory canon, helped Eric out of his anxiety and guilt. This is not to say that those two exceptional reverends did not fall into church code of belief on the rule of the devil. But they at least were equally concerned with the psychological well-being of a young man within their ministry.

Eric also convinced his parents to pay for psychotherapy, ostensibly for his speech defect. In fact, he underwent analysis that relieved him of the stutter in his soul. Years after the night at the movies, I ran into Eric during a visit to my hometown. I knew he had become a schoolteacher—of world religions. He was happily married with two small children, and he spoke without a trace of mumbling and with quiet confidence. We laughed about our milestone night at the movies. I asked him, "How did you really get out of that rut?"

He responded: "I decided to argue with it."

IN ORDER TO MAKE a bed with your religious tradition, you must struggle with it from time to time. The very name, "Israel," means "the one who wrestles with angels." You have to stand up, even to God or those who claim to represent God. The preachers won't often tell you, because it threatens their authority, that this is a key fabric in the biblical tapestry. As we shall see, every true leader, prophet, and spiritualist of every faith has argued with fate and with God—from Sarah to Moses to Jesus to Martin Luther King, Jr.

It is obvious that uncompromising religious obeisance is the source of most every deadly conflict now blazing in this world. A religious crusade, of any kind, has nothing to do with the human spirit and everything to do with tyranny. Violence is not only physical; there is spiritual violence that turns growing children into cowering, angst-ridden misfits and that corrupts righteous clerics into bloodthirsty warlords. My boyhood chum Eric did not suffer from such persons but he did suffer from such sanctimoniousness.

Being a rabbi, a pastor, or an imam is not about power. It is about possibility. That is something you cannot only believe but you should demand.

When my friend Eric began to argue with the God he was presented with in church, he was merely emulating Jesus. Pastor Ken Silva has written about a verse in the Gospel of Mark: Jesus said to them, "Is this not the reason you are wrong, because you know neither the Scriptures nor the power of God?" Jesus's entire ministry was an argument with the status quo, with what he perceived as a calcified, insensitive, despotic religious pecking order that confused insulation with inspiration. Silva isn't too happy either with the modern state of affairs in the Christian hierarchy and he summarizes his distress succinctly: "It's only because the visible church, fearful of conflict, has decided to follow the whimsical ways of our effete culture that Christ's confrontational style has been hidden."

Christ's confrontational style. I'm not a Christian, but I like that. Religion works best when it's not telling you what to think but when it's exhorting you *to think.* In my lifetime, I heard our nation's first Catholic president, the young John F. Kennedy, close his Inaugural Address on a bitter cold day in Washington, January 20, 1961, by exclaiming: "God's work on Earth must truly be our own." Yes, we are God's partners, not God's slaves. You can find the proof of this right in the Bible.

Sarah, the mother of monotheism, argued with God. Noah failed at this. Abraham sometimes did and sometimes didn't—the Jewish tradition is critical and concerned about his inconsistencies. The very greatness of Moses and his high rank among all the Western religions is exactly because he was an independent, cantankerous spiritual legislator who argued with God when he thought God was wrong.

Let's see how these individuals, all sanctified in religious tradition, did when it came to arguing with God and how their stories can help us know what to believe.

Sarah, like many women, sought to bear a child. She wanted to be a mom. (The Bible spends much more time exploring the pains, joys, yearnings, and anguishes of the people in the narrative than it does portraying the big miracles.) Her husband, Abraham, had children via handmaids and concubines, a routine practice in that time and place. The Bible doesn't sidestep Sarah's heavy heart as she becomes postmenopausal. It doesn't whitewash her resentment—even cruelty—toward a favorite sexual partner of Abraham's named Hagar. Banished to the desert, thirsty and scorched by sun and sand, Hagar clutched her newborn son Ishmael—the primal beacon figure of Islam.

Whatever is happening in the Muslim world today, the Hebrew Bible unequivocally anoints Abraham's son Ishmael with special status: "I will multiply thy seed exceedingly." In other words, Ishmael's descendants will become a great nation. Here is a rebuttal of blanket Islamophobia.

Meanwhile, in a classic tale of sexism, three mysterious men ("divine messengers") appear at Abraham's tent flap and tell the old man that he and Sarah will bear a son together after all. Sarah happens to overhear "the boys" discussing her body and her sexual promise from within the tent. Mystified, defiant, joyous, and indignant, Sarah laughed out loud. To paraphrase her infamous muttering found in the Book of Genesis about this locker room moment, Sarah said to herself: "Right. I'm going to have a kid at my age. And with my old husband."

According to the legend, God heard Sarah's little blasphemy and became quite vexed. The God of the early Bible had a number of anger management issues, as we shall see. In keeping with the shameless paternalism of this story, God went straight to Abraham and asked, "Why did Sarah laugh? Is anything too hard for the Lord?"

I feel this segment of scripture was written by men who didn't want anyone, especially a woman, to question God. Even when what God proposes is a biological impossibility. It's not that different from the long-standing antagonism of organized religious groups toward women's rights and access to prayer, study, and even careers in the clergy. What if Sarah hadn't argued with heaven, hadn't stood up to male insecurity, hadn't been bold, and had simply submitted to "God's will"? Would the countless, valiant campaigns and movements for women's freedoms, for suffrage, for equal pay have retained an original biblical role model? Would the teenage Pakistani education activist Malala Yousafzai, shot in the face by a Taliban gunman, have a scriptural mentor and go on to win the 2014 Nobel Peace Prize?

All Sarah wanted was to bear a child with her husband and to have the attention and respect of that husband. What she wound up doing was teaching us that before you can believe in God, you have to believe in yourself.

And what of Abraham? Was he a leader with God or a lackey for God? It depends upon where you look in the Bible. Like almost anybody, including you and me, Abraham was filled with contradictions that he reacted to and felt varying levels of motivation about things at several points in his life. It's just like you and me: On Monday, we don't believe in God. On Tuesday, we do. When we were teenagers, we were immortal and unassailable and didn't really stress about God and prayers and fate. Older and frailer, we need to care. But we also need to think and sort out what works for us, what comforts us, as our friends and family die off and we are looking down the tunnel of mortality.

There is the well-known story of Abraham trying to convince God not to destroy the wicked cities of Sodom and Gomorrah. Here was a double village of depravity and debauchery and our hero is actually bargaining with God not to destroy it. Abraham pleads, "What if there are fifty good people in the city? Will you spare it for fifty good souls?" Okay, God agrees; for fifty good and pure folks, it will be saved. Abraham pushes the envelope: What if there are forty good ones? All right, God agrees; forty. Abraham keeps up the bartering. It goes down to thirty and then to twenty. He and God finally settle at ten. If there were ten virtuous people to be found in Sodom and Gomorrah, the entire place remains standing. (A Jewish tradition asserts that this final numeral in the negotiation, ten, became the minimum number of people required to form a *minyan*—a group large enough to have a religious service.)

Unfortunately, there weren't even ten upstanding individuals in that miserable community and it was wiped out. But the story, found right in the heart of the Bible, effectively indicates that if you see a possible injustice or you don't understand what God (or God's theologians) is disseminating, then you are supposed to speak out. God did not create us to simply fall in line. We were created to be God's partners. Heaven is not tyranny; heaven is hope.

Yet later, Abraham strangely goes mute when God commands him to do something unthinkable: "Take your son Isaac (the only child Abraham produced with Sarah), your son that you love, go up to Mount Moriah, and offer him there for a burnt-offering upon the mountain."

Really? Abraham is supposed to kill and sacrifice his teenage boy to God? Well, after the commotion Abraham put up to save a city of criminals, the man will surely argue with this crazy notion! Look in Genesis, chapter 22, and see Abraham's response. Not a word. Not a single protest. Here's the verse that follows immediately after God's outlandish request:

And Abraham rose up early in the morning and saddled his ass and took two of his young men with him, and Isaac his son, and collected wood for the burnt-offering, and rose up, and went to the place of which God had told him.

Centuries of anguished scholarship, rationalization, and dispute have failed to mitigate or explain away how a preeminent seer of Western theology did not utter a syllable of protest when God instructs him to slaughter his own child.

Of course we know Abraham did not ultimately do that terrible thing. But not because he didn't intend do. He had the fire blazing and the blade up in the air to slay the boy and was only stayed by the intervention of an "angel of God." It was a test, a loyalty check to evaluate just how faithful Abraham really was to this deity: "Lay not thy hand upon the lad, neither do anything to him. For now I know that thou fearest God, seeing that thou has not withheld thy son." A ram was substituted; God was going to get something out of this strange little trial of allegiance.

Anybody who knows this story and is honest with him- or herself has thought the same thing: *I don't know what to believe.* The story begins to be comprehensible, fathomable, and even acceptable (as opposed to being repugnant) only when we start questioning it. It's not enough that the Jewish doctrine on this claims that it teaches people not to sacrifice their children. People continue to sacrifice their kids all the time—to wars, abuse, addiction, trafficking, and neglect. The story has no moral possibilities if we just believe in it. It only has ethical value or spiritual merit if we argue with it, and that is what you can believe.

And then there was Noah.

It's worth noting that Noah of the Bible was neither a Jew nor a Christian nor affiliated with any organized creed. I mention this because of the frequent co-opting of his story and that of the global flood (or total genocide, if you look at it for what it was) by clergy people in the name of their faiths. Noah was an unassuming man who, according to the writ, was selected by God to build an ark and save his family along with "two of every kind" from the animal kingdom. This is perhaps the most renowned tale of all time and the destruction of humanity by a cataclysmic deluge appears as a parable in other ancient literatures, including from Babylonia, Egypt, and Africa. Most all of these traditions also showcase a boat and feature returning, redemptive birds—like the dove in the Genesis account that returns with a green leaf and some hope.

What were Noah's credentials for this assignment according to Genesis? He was not a seer, an oracle, or even a nautical expert. He wasn't exactly Billy Graham or Nelson Mandela. All Genesis tells us is that Noah was "a righteous man in his time."

A righteous man in his time? What was "his time"? In terms of human behavior, this was a period of history so desperately bleak and despicable that the Bible summarizes it in one succinct sentence: "The earth was corrupt before God and the earth was filled with violence." In fact, the scripture intimates that God was thoroughly disgusted with the human beings he had created and that the entire demographic of the planet amounted to a bunch of hedonists, rakes, thieves, rapists, and degenerates. Against that standard, Noah was the best. This is not a ringing endorsement of Noah's character or standards. He was all God had to work with.

You don't have to believe the whole story; it's a shared myth of many civilizations, and it does have a powerful and meaningful ethical message. What you can take away from this very drenched business is that greatness is relative to the period being examined. Noah happened not to be a total debaucher. So in his time he stood out. We could use some of this perspective in our current era of celebrity worship, narcissism, and sycophants. Better than deifying Noah—or any of the highly flawed human heroes of the biblical literature—we should remember their "greatness" is always to be defined against the reality of their circumstances, as well as their own human frailties.

When we beatify well-known people or even private individuals in our lives, from parents to popes to ballplayers to media icons, we will inevitably wind up hurt, disillusioned, and confused.

Here's something you can believe when it comes to people, theology, miracles, and psaltery: The answer is always somewhere in between. There is somewhere you can alight in between atheism and evangelism and even that point of landing will—and must—fluctuate as you pass through the triumphs, setbacks, illnesses, recoveries, crises, and renewals of this thing called life.

When it comes to the flood phenomenon, for example, don't get drowned in the torrent. In general, don't get stuck on miracles. You and I are not angels, saints, or demigods. We are people. We get scared, hungry, sick, angry, unhappy, divorced, and we are mystified and threatened by life's incongruities. We battle with our weight. We dread cancer. We fall out of love. We make mistakes and we damage other folks, unwittingly or not. We have nightmares and we suffer the effects of family dysfunction. We struggle with demons. We are dismayed and shaken as we notice our parents weakening, stumbling, and forgetting in old age. We drive by a cemetery in the afternoon and try to subdue the dark grip of mortality on our hearts. We bury our parents there, our brothers, sisters, and sometimes our children. Their open graves leave gaping holes in our hearts. Don't we scream at God, dispute with God, and even condemn God at such moments of incredulity? So shouldn't religion offer a valve for such inevitable apoplexies of the spirit?

We are usually doing the best we can in a world whose madness is broadcast and cyber-blasted into our heads twenty-four/seven and the last thing we need is an authoritarian lecture or a devotional booklet telling us that unless we act or think in this or that way, we are doomed, going to hell, or will generally suffer the disapproval of God Almighty. We get enough of that without even going to church.

Again, the text is not our homeland; life is.

Better you should stick to the measured human insight that a man's or a woman's "greatness" (and the assumed gospel-wisdom of a spiritual dignitary) are all measured against what's going on around that person. And it is suckled by the naïveté and/or insecurity of those of us who cling to these champions. Believe in yourself before you surrender your faith to the anointed. Remember the devotional manual offers us answers, but we have the questions and these don't always match up perfectly.

Meanwhile, Noah was a faithful tool in this drama, but he was not so great at all. The genuinely great ones argue with fate—especially when fate threatens human life.

God hones in on Noah and tells him "the end of all flesh is before me" and God is going to wipe out every form of life on the planet. Not a particular nation, tribe, city, or subdivision. Everybody is going down. Noah, build an ark.

What is Noah's response to this astonishing report? Nothing. No protest, no debate. Basically, it's "What are the measurements of the craft, what kind of wood should I use?" Noah just listens to a divine blueprint involving gopher wood, pitch, and the precise number of cubits. Oh, and there's to be a single window. And a large side door. Get going, man. The rain is coming. And God also declares he is making "a covenant" with Noah—only his family and the saved wildlife will survive and that's the deal.

The Bible tells us bluntly: "Thus Noah did." Good man follows instructions, but this is not a candidate for induction into the Hall of Greatness. It clearly took Noah and his offspring a significant amount of time to construct the big boat. This was done out in the open sunlight, and it can be presumed that passers-by noticed all the busy work ongoing, heard the mallets and saws being used, not to mention the long procession of paired giraffes, elephants, apes, goats, cows, cheetahs, boa constrictors, possums, turkeys, alligators, geese, squirrels, peacocks, and warthogs making their way onto the platform.

Even the rabbinic commentary on this episode lambasts Noah for not reaching out to a single person, warning them to change their ways, repent, or at least seek higher ground! Nor are the more progressive biblical sages particularly impressed with Noah's absolute, wordless compliance with God's horrific intentions. Maybe the man just focused on "the covenant" God offered him and chose to be utterly selfish and thoroughly ordinary.

Not so with Moses, a flawed man like anybody else except when it came to looking out for others before saving his own skin. Atop Mt. Sinai, alone and literally burning in the light of God's countenance, about to receive the Ten Commandments, Moses gets a real twist in the conversation with the Almighty: "Get thee down, for thy people which thou brought out of Egypt, have corrupted themselves."

Moses listens as God excoriates the Hebrews below for ditching all their jewelry and gold and building "a molten calf," which amounts to an abominable idol-god. They are praying to this golden calf and offering it sacrifices. I've seen it, Moses, and these people are nothing but a bunch of ungrateful, stiff-necked hacks! The Bible makes it quite clear that God is in a livid meltdown and he's out to kill again.

"Now, therefore let me alone, that my wrath may wax hot against them, and that I may consume them. And I will make of thee a great nation."

In other words: Don't try to talk me out of this; I need to vent my spleen; I need to wipe these flunkies out. And then God throws in the same "covenant" deal to Moses that he offered Noah. Basically, God will start all over again with Moses as the progenitor. Although in this case, God is killing Hebrews exclusively, not dunking the whole Earth and the entirety of creation.

How does Moses react? First of all, he reacts. Completely disregarding the offer of his own lineal covenant, Moses responds: "Why are you so furious with your people that you freed from Egypt with such great authority and a mighty hand? What will the Egyptians say? That you freed them just to destroy them?" And then, with unabashed chutzpah, Moses actually challenges God: "Turn from your fierce wrath and repent of this evil against your people."

Whenever you pray (and it doesn't matter where you pray), aren't you negotiating with God? It's important to know that Moses—who had a pretty successful career as a rabbi and civil rights leader—regularly contended with God about what Moses thought was right. Even if what God was doling out appeared wrong. This is what you can believe: A relationship with God is not about simply acquiescing to heaven. It's about arguing with fate and eternity and angels and even with God. Sometimes religion helps us to accomplish this, especially when it's not skewed by the arrogance and self-importance of its leaders or the dogmas of its liturgies. All of these kinds of things are readily serviced by our understandable fears and insecurities, and sometimes preachers and cultists feed off them.

Religion should not take advantage of us. It should take us home. And the way home is discovered along the path of a vibrant and, yes, contentious spirituality. You can look this up in the Bible.

It turns out that Moses completely convinces God to spare the Hebrews. By lowering the temperature on top of that mountain, by exhibiting some spiritual muscle, Moses saved religion for that day.

Chapter Four

THE RULES SOMETIMES GET IN THE WAY

"The Bible was not given to angels."
—THE TALMUD

WHAT THE ANCIENT RABBIS meant by this insightful declaration, this expression in favor of human intellect and creativity, is simple: Scripture (*Torah* in Hebrew) wasn't meant for implementation in heaven; it only works in the imperfect world of human life. That means even scripture has to bend to the ebb and flow of our tough and vital experiences as people. Just like us, the characters in the Bible are confronted by many unforeseen circumstances: They fight with their kids; they fall in love; they bury their dead; and they struggle through faith crises. And they didn't have any divinity books to consult. They managed on their own wits, savvy, and spirits.

Look out into the crowd you walk through in the mall or on a downtown street; the folks you pass are just like the people in the Bible, they are strangers with stories.

In another Talmudic gem, the sages wrote: "If all you have is Torah, then you don't even have Torah." How intuitive and wonderful is that? In other words, if all you do is proclaim and stay locked in the writ, then you've missed the point and you've lost the writ. Therefore, scripture (according to its most zealous advocates and interpreters) doesn't fly unless it's carried aloft and adjusts to the winds and whims of our existences as human persons. We have to adapt to hard situations and sudden calamities. People die in Florida but their cemetery plots are back home in Connecticut. Their survivors are not (this applies to the Jewish community that has traditionally required burial within twenty-four hours) going to achieve interment by the next day. But that does not mean the dead are going to be forgotten.

And now comes the starry-eyed couple who wants to celebrate their wedding ceremony on a Saturday evening. If traditional Jewish observance is at play, then they would not be able to enjoy their feast until 10:00 P.M. or later during the spring and summer months after a 9:00 or 9:30 P.M. nuptial because they can't have it until the Jewish Sabbath is completely over. That means at least three stars are visible in the evening sky. Really? Are we more stuck on such literalism than we are moved by love?

We need to bend outmoded laws, given the new modalities. Not to discard the laws. And certainly not to wantonly dispose of meaningful rituals. They enrich both the joyous and bittersweet milestone moments. But they should not devour such moments. The Bible was written long before refrigeration and sanitary standards modified the strict urgency of dietary laws and before mechanized and jet transportation altered our demographic relationship with these edicts.

The old laws should still make you think about what you put in your mouth, what we all should do to conserve good harvesting soil, clean air, and a fair distribution of food to a planet plagued with hungry children. If you are Jewish and keep kosher or you are Christian and don't consume meat on Fridays or Muslim and don't eat pork, that's truly commendable. It just needs to be more than a bunch of feel-good pieties.

If you do such things but are indifferent about poverty or immoral in your community values, then what's the difference if your daughter gets married exactly after sundown on Saturday evening or if you support your church on Sunday morning while rationalizing the intermittent hypocrisies and felonies of your ordained church leaders?

People are buried, married, and even circumcised throughout the scriptural narrative. In no case is a specific day or time of day invoked—what resonates is the spiritual impact of these rites. The Sabbath day is certainly venerated and structured in the Torah; both Christianity and Islam have adopted its concepts of rest, renewal, and creativity on Sunday and Friday, respectively. The Old Testament specifies that one should not work on the Sabbath. How does a ban on "work" conceived by a nomadic desert people four thousand years ago transfer into an injunction against driving your Toyota to visit your grandchildren on a Saturday afternoon?

We need the safety valve of spiritual honesty to service and liberate the old texts from the dust of their ancient caverns. Truth is portable as sure as the sun and the moon are in constant motion. Life is a river of informative situations and mysteries but only when the river is not frozen. It needs the heat of the sun as surely as we need the warmth of pastoral kindness. Judaism and Christianity both assert that the ultimate law, the supreme concept, is "love thy neighbor." Compared to this nonjudgmental, peace-seeking idea, the rest of the text is commentary. And it is vulnerable to manipulation by clerics or cultists who have forgotten about love and just have a need to control.

Every religion survives not because of its restrictions, but via its freedoms. When people dictate what you think and do and the intent is to supervise your soul, invariably there will be a problem. Liturgies and laws aspire to line up things into some kind of order that can be helpful, especially when certain rituals link you to the past and help you walk to the future. The reality is that life rarely lines up itself; it is not a grid and it does fall into place neatly.

When I remember my relatives and friends who have died, I surely recite what the Jews call the "Mourner's Kaddish." This old Aramaic prayer (most Jews mistakenly assume it's in Hebrew) joins me to my parents and other elders and some departed young people as well because it links my grief to a calendar cycle—and that's fine. But if I just voice the Kaddish as a procedural and then resume my business, not much has really happened. Religion is grammar, but spirituality is language. Religion is words; spirituality is love.

When I remember my dad while saying the Kaddish, *really remember him*, then I'm thinking about his deep brown eyes, his magnetic smile, his strong hands, and, yes, his flights of anger. I think about him, and therefore he lives. I can hear his voice. His soul has wings. A prayer that is felt and not just spoken is a chance to visit with somebody.

A death certainly needs an organized response. But it *requires* pain, bewailing, listening, and our agony cannot be managed into a box. It also needs the unbound therapy of grief, which is as personal and multifaceted as the way people die and when they die. Meanwhile, we, their survivors, also cope with the tyranny of mortality—the prevailing sadness of human life.

The only constant is that we all die. While we are living and dealing with the dead, we cannot be administered by a rote formula; there is no such thing. That would be the equivalent of asserting that every person who has died was not utterly unique, or that we each contemplate and fear death identically. There must be safety valves laid into the religious constructions or we shall be further afflicted by the harsh realism of someone's death rather than grow with the experience.

At the end of the day, religion was created as a response to death; spirituality is about creating a response to life. Nobody has ever said to me after losing a loved one, "I feel her religion here with me." What I hear is "I feel her spirit here with me."

LITTLE BEN WAS TEN years old when he hung himself above his bunk bed in Portsmouth, Ohio. While there is no face value in the comparison, the fact that the sheepish, freckle-faced boy ended his painfully short lifetime came to change my spiritual life forever. This dreadful event, combined with some trying logistics concerning Ben's burial, led me to a decision that has defined my relationship with God for all times.

Ben's parents, Stephen and Angela, were comfortable and prosperous in Portsmouth, a rust-belt town at the southeastern tip of the state, across from West Virginia and bounded by the Scioto and Ohio Rivers. The economically hard-pressed community of abandoned steel mills and nearby Indian mounds nonetheless included a neatly maintained Jewish temple of some twenty-five families. Stephen, a successful and well-liked dentist, was president of the synagogue during my stint as the biweekly "student-rabbi" from 1976 to 1978. I drove 120 miles from Cincinnati to the town along the scenic river route, US 52, every second Friday afternoon.

Stephen and Angela resided in a hilly suburban enclave of imposing homes some distance from the rather blighted downtown. He was a man of rugged looks, angular and fit. She was pretty; her face and cheeks were round and soft. Angela was a nurse who had converted to Judaism and they partnered well in raising three outwardly good-natured children—of whom Ben was the youngest. Because of the coincidence of our first names, I dubbed him "Little Ben."

On the surface, the family appeared healthy and happy, living a life of affluence and creature comforts within the bubble of their shady neighborhood of chestnut and maple trees, winding roads, remote-controlled three-car garages, aluminum fences, brick walls, and sophisticated security systems. It turned out that, behind the walls, Little Ben was struggling with demons and mental health issues.

During my tenure as student-rabbi, I grew close to the family, often dining in their home and celebrating festive occasions. All five of them were in attendance at my ordination as a rabbi in 1978. I went on to my first posting, in Toronto, with fond recollections of the household.

The phone call came to me almost two years later. It was a neighbor, also a member of the temple. Ben had taken his own life; his parents found him hanging lifeless and were in a state of catatonic shock. Would I please come down to Portsmouth to help and conduct their boy's funeral?

Ben committed suicide on a Thursday. The demanding Jewish clock started ticking. However, Friday appeared too soon to bury him because many people, including me, had to travel and gather around the family. If we did not have the funeral on Saturday, we'd have to wait until Monday because the local cemetery did not bury on Sunday due to union regulations, as I sadly learned. This cultural tension about entombing the dead within a day was gnawing at an already surreal and ghastly situation.

My father had died, suddenly, just three years earlier. He dropped dead on a handball court at about 6:00 P.M. on a Tuesday. Even in my own shock, I could not grasp the urgency—imposed by our jocular but strict Orthodox rabbi—to put my father in the ground at 2:00 P.M. the next day.

Would one more day have made a difference? Yes; a bevy of my desired and dear friends and relatives would have arrived in time to emotionally support me and all of our family over the gaping hole of my father's untimely grave. Instead, they were only able to join us for deli, coffee, and perfunctory prayers in our teeming home overstrained by crowds and gossip.

Now in Portsmouth, one thing became obvious: Friday was too soon and abrupt. Yet waiting till Monday was just going to be too painful for Ben's family and many folks would have returned home by then. It was a classic tension that compelled spiritual pragmatism.

Ben's mother and father needed both reasonable time and sensible closure. A close friend of the family, an exceptionally kind Christian man, said to me, "That boy has to be buried tomorrow." *Saturday?* I trembled. Saturday is the Jewish Sabbath, when funerals are generally forbidden; however, I did not reject the notion. I thought God would be more interested in the empathy and pragmatism behind such a decision than in the time-honored injunction of rapidity. In my mind and heart, I broached the possibility of a funeral on the Jewish Sabbath.

I have made this kind of judgment over and over again since then: to choose love over religion or at least to draw them equivalent. The writ is not what we live; it's what we study. Like my father and his army comrades back in Israel, I believe in God but also assert that we need tools in order to cope with what God sends us. As the renowned Christian scholar Karen Armstrong, a former nun, has written: "I say that religion isn't about believing things. It's about what you do. It's ethical alchemy. It's about behaving in a way that changes you, that gives you intimations of holiness and sacredness."

The benign God, who continued to whisper in my ear after Little Ben died, and I broke some sacrosanct rules to mitigate the crisis is the

God I pray to now. This is the God who speaks to me in clear terms that transcend liturgies, and the one who understands the great peace in my heart.

This hardly means that I'm not fully ingrained with my Judaism. I became a bar mitzvah under the rigorous but loving tutelage of an Orthodox rabbi whose memory I bless, came through the pangs of adolescence via the Conservative Jewish youth movement, and was ordained by the Reform (Liberal) Jewish movement. I was born—and my parents are buried—in Israel. I know all the liturgies, pray with all the prayer books, and have led others in theological study around the world. In the end, I am just a Jew, filled with the biblical spirit of inclusiveness, more in need of natural holiness than contrived piety, thoroughly not in the need of anybody's approval.

I loved it when, one night several years ago, the kindhearted Imam of San Diego introduced me at an Islamic-Jewish conference with the declaration: "I yield, naturally, to one who represents the oldest faith, the one that first taught us that God is simply there, however we call out to him."

So the first time I realized that not all the religious directives necessarily apply to every situation was when Little Ben took his own life. The awkward, brown-eyed boy put a rope around his neck in his bedroom— unfathomable. The reasons were, of course, multifarious and fearsome; what was clear above everything was his young family, parents, older brother, and sister, were unalterably afflicted and needed support. They needed that more than sanctimony.

The fact that Ben's family remains intact and quite well-adjusted more than thirty years later, and that they survived this catastrophe and are raising a third generation and celebrating holidays and milestones is great tribute to the love they share. That love, for tragically clinical and predisposed reasons, failed to heal Ben's congenital neuroses. But his family, together and individually, have made their own deal with God.

A blended kin of both Jewish and Christian legacies, they have thankfully found some comfort in rituals. They also have been aided by other forms of solace and relief via unrestricted prayer and nondoctrinal therapies. Judaism has been their river of healing to a sea of ideas and devotions ranging from Apache poems to Hindu philosophies to Christian hymns to Hebrew psalms.

They just sought one God when they cried for their little boy; the fire in their souls did not distinguish among denominations. "Be still, and know that I am God," it is written in Psalms—for anyone who was ever a human being and has suffered.

For a while after losing Ben, his parents and siblings carried a white-hot anger and a drenching guilt that no ecclesiastical platitudes could have borne. That Friday when I arrived, they were reeling in the primal stages of grief and disbelief: "Why us, Rabbi Ben? We loved him so much. We gave so much time to the temple, and we celebrated the Jewish holidays and visited the sick and supported the charities. Why did God let this happen to us?"

There was no published formula or organization in their eventual recovery, only a redeeming amalgam of pain, time, and reality. They did some of their grieving within organized religious settings, more of it in their own ways. No one who really believes in God could have stood by in judgment. Wherever they got help—that was good, that was God.

But on that terrible Friday, we had a real challenge, and it welled up in our faces even as the steam of grief filled every room, every hallway, and every crevice. When I arrived around ten in the morning, the impact of the suicide was still cutting into each greeting and every discussion. The family alternately wept, pounded on tables, stared at one another in stone silence. Neighbors and friends, clutching their own children like life itself, dutifully spoke in hushed tones, arranged place settings, delivered unwanted food, made genuine if stiff attempts to console the mourners. The family's home was filled with helplessness and the smell of coffee. So, when would the funeral and burial take place?

My first thought, of course, was that we do it on Sunday. I heard a few people ask me, "Aren't you going to perform the service today? There's still time before the Sabbath." Only a myopic fundamentalist would drag this family through the brutal ritual so abruptly in order to fulfill some conventional dictate that had little to do with the emotional and practical realities. Long ago, when the Jews clustered together in tents and villages, separated or ghettoized, then it perhaps made sense to bury within twenty-four hours. Nobody, especially Ben's immediate family, could even let out a breath on that shattering Friday of reality and delayed shock— they hadn't even chosen a casket for their child at the nonsectarian local mortuary.

I began to actively consider: Saturday, the next day, might be ideal, a balance of compromise and sensibilities. But the Sabbath prohibition and even the potential professional stigma pulled at me. So Sunday was the answer, I initially supposed, and such a weekend interval is normal in today's world. In truth, most rabbis, but for the fundamentalists, allow two days to elapse out of the considerations of common sense.

"Well, you can't do it on Sunday, Rabbi," the funeral director told me, with solicitousness and concern. "The cemetery is closed and there are no gravediggers to work."

"Well, can't you make an exception? This situation is extraordinary, as you can see. You know the family." I pleaded with the man, gasping at the thought of making Ben's mother wait until Monday for the closure of burial. As much as we could not pull the ceremony off immediately, on that Friday, it seemed just as punishing to stay the ceremony till Monday.

"I'd like to help," he said. "But it's a union thing. We simply can't have them working on Sundays. It's contracted and we'd be raising hell."

"Don't many of those men have children?" I asked, trying hard not to be argumentative, but in a rising panic over this developing predicament.

"We can do it tomorrow or we can do it Monday. I'm sorry, Rabbi, but that's the way it is."

Oh God, what do I do?

Not comparing my own professional anguish over timing to the family's unspeakable agony over their lost boy, I writhed in despair and confusion nonetheless. I was young then and new at this. I was still honed in by old ghosts, stern Hebrew school teachers, unyielding rabbis pounding on pulpits, the imprint of prayer books I held as a youth, the waning hot wax of holiday candles, and the ancient smell of Torah scrolls being marched by me in ancestral ceremonials. The last thing we were ever told was to improvise; the first thing we were instructed was to follow the edicts even when history and fate were not bending to those edicts.

I knew it was basically unheard of, even a sacrilege, to perform a Jewish funeral on Saturday. I turned to the family for a sense of their feeling. Even from the depths of their grief, they understood my dilemma but gently pleaded on that Friday for a ceremony tomorrow, please tomorrow. They had little tolerance for rules and rituals. What they also knew was that they could not keep their dead son above ground until Monday; that such a wait would be intolerable, and perhaps I should carefully examine the situation and come up with the answer.

They also had the practical problem of certain family and friends, dear support people who were already on the scene but would have to depart before Monday. The fact is that a burial without familiar kin who were present or on their way—Ben's grandparents, this uncle, or that cherished college friend—would actually be terrifying. The family, like any distraught, guilt-ridden household, needed the tenderness and support of recognizable faces. Save for tradition, Saturday now seemed ideal in the midst of this nightmare.

But how would I rationalize a funeral on the Sabbath—such a revered exclusion? Where would I find the balance between the overpowering convention and the screaming practicality?

I thought, *Have the Jews not always survived by their flexibility and adaptability? Who's to say, really, what was right and what was wrong in this situation? What was more urgent, the parents' need to grieve as expediently as possible or the overall Jewish grieving ritual itself? Whose endurance was actually at stake—the family's or the Jewish community's?*

I retired to my hotel room for some time to reflect and decided to seek the advice of a more seasoned rabbinic colleague in the area. I was able to get through to a senior rabbi in one of the state's major congregations. I did not know him personally, but needed help and some consolation. The reaction I got was strong and fixated: Under no circumstances can you bury that kid tomorrow. The Sabbath is the Sabbath. They'll just have to wait till Monday if you can't do it Sunday. Good luck, Kamin. Don't forget who's in charge.

The rabbi did not have much patience for my inquiry altogether. I wondered what he would really do if he were in my shoes in that moment in that place. I prayed to God for the guidance I had not received from a fellow clergyman.

I sat and thought things out in the Ramada Inn in Portsmouth, Ohio. I prayed some more—no prayer book, just my own deep and personal supplications. I even rationalized the timing issue: Saturday afternoon in Portsmouth, Ohio would already be late Saturday evening—or after the Sabbath—in Jerusalem. Well, that was trite, I realized. What really mattered, it finally resolved for me, were the issues of compassion and common sense; the same fusion that has sustained Jewish life specifically and spiritual life generally across many centuries and many much greater difficulties and dilemmas.

Okay, I needed to look something up in the Bible. Pulling the bedside drawer open, I grabbed the ubiquitous King James edition, but it looked absolutely holy and splendid to me. We all have the same fears and suffer the same needs. I turned to the account in Genesis of the first funeral described in scripture—that of Sarah. Abraham outlived his strong-minded wife; now he had to tend to her final rites. He did not call a preacher or refer to a manual:

And Abraham came to mourn for her, weep for her, and eulogize her.

There it was: my answer. There was no calendar, and there were no regulations invoked in the account. The text doesn't mention a given day in the week. It just states, with a certain elegiac music, that someone died and that person's loved one came to cry and to say good-bye. Surely, some kind of ritual was involved but the old writ was speaking to me beyond all that and in the language of pure spirituality. One reads it and is touched by the love and not fazed by the law.

Without further fanfare, and without even alluding to my personal quandary, I returned to the family home and began making plans for the funeral the next day. I felt God's palm on my shoulder—sometimes pressing, sometimes stroking. But of one thing I was absolutely certain, deep within myself: This family needed to move forward and bury the dead and then continue through the various passages of mourning and woe. The Sabbath and the Jewish people would endure this tender transgression in the name of reason.

I have never stopped thinking about the decision I made that weekend in Portsmouth, Ohio, but I have never regretted it either. I believe in a compassionate God who is more interested in healing a family than in avenging a sacrament. I believe Little Ben's family was better affected by a reasoned adjustment to reality than to stubborn obeisance to a rite that more than survived our small remedial alteration.

Ben's brother and sister are successful, middle-aged professionals now, both married and with their own children. Stephen and Angela took the Yiddish nicknames of "Bubbe" and "Zeyde" (Grandma and Grandpa), watched their two living children get married, and then frolicked with their grandkids. They left the declining Portsmouth and relocated to Florida. They defied the 90 percent odds that couples who have lost a child eventually divorce. Stephen succumbed to cancer in his mid-sixties, but Angela continues to regale her generations as the matriarch of a large family circle.

Little Ben's bones lie in the ground on a slope in southeastern Ohio, alternately covered by dogwood leaves, snow, marigolds, dandelions, and then drenched by summer rains. Nobody reminisces about how much Hebrew was spoken or chanted the day the boy was laid to rest. Not a single person was compelled to judge anybody else that day. Few likely recall that it was a Saturday. They just remember that it was a day much more about broken hearts than running clocks.

The Bible was not given to angels. Angels don't die.

Chapter Five

SPIRITUALITY SOFTENS
THE CONTRADICTIONS

*"The most virtuous jihad is when one speaks
a word of truth before an unjust ruler."*
—Mohammed

How do you deal with the fact that scripture contains mistakes and inconsistencies?

Teddy Kollek, then the bellicose mayor of Jerusalem, was in a phone booth in the lobby of the city's Marriott Tower Hotel, his bulk and personality filling the cramped space as he screamed into the receiver. It was 1983, and I was the young New York director of an international Jewish agency dedicated to help spread religious pluralism, that is, tolerance, in Israel and other countries. I needed the mayor to finish his animated discussion with the party on the end of the line because he, Mayor Kollek, was already several minutes late for his presentation at our international plenum.

Almost a thousand liberal theologians and lay leaders were waiting and Kollek was still bellowing and pounding on the phone booth door while paying me no heed. I tapped on the glass. Kollek looked up at me with blazing eyes of annoyance and then stuck his large head out for a moment. "What?" His voice boomed across the noisy lobby. I told him what. He gathered himself for a second and his eyes sent me a message of begrudging acknowledgment.

"Okay, okay. I'll finish this call now and be right over. They can wait a little. In Jerusalem, everybody waits for the truth even though they think they already own it."

Several hours later, after Teddy Kollek captivated our conference with his vision of a Jerusalem that treated and serviced the entirety of its churning demographics with equanimity, that provided equal education and safe streets to the Armenian, Jewish, Muslim, and Christian Quarters, I asked the mayor who he was yelling at in the phone booth prior to the session.

"A goddam dairy distributor I know in the western section." Kollek barked while referring to the newer, predominately Jewish side of the city. We were sharing some scotch and the big man was uncharacteristically mellow—if only for a moment. "I told him that a group of Arab mothers had come to see me. They weren't getting the milk deliveries we in the municipality promised them. I hate that! We Jews cannot claim to administer the entire city unless the Arab baby gets the same fresh milk the Jewish baby gets in the morning. In Jerusalem, baby's milk is foreign policy."

Jerusalem is a city like any other, only more so, and from politics to piety, much more so. Its golden light, reflecting off its domes and bleaching its hills, hangs in the air like in no other place; history's running blood in its arched stony streets flows like a river of zealotry that quenches the thirst of madmen. This city is a source of consecration that has been tragically outsourced by Christian crusaders murderously blinded by their faith, by "Torah-true" Jews ensnared by their religious atrophy, and by caliphs who order murder. There is no quantitative analysis here. The issue is not how many people the Christians have killed, how many the Jews, or how many the Muslims. The issue is that all these clerics have killed God.

Jerusalem is the place where the sky begins. It is the eternal village where heaven arcs into Earth but also the site of the greatest, ongoing cataclysmic disaster on this planet. The bleeding intersection of too many overlapping beliefs, Jerusalem is, to my mind, the best argument for choosing spiritual liberty over religious intimidation. I've seen things there that affirm my belief in the one God—we humans are the troublemakers who disturb the peace of the celestials. We humans devised these religions, not God.

The city, reunited by Israel during the Six Day War in June of 1967, is seething with judgment. Rarely do any of its three tribes, the Jews, the Christians, and the Muslims miss an opportunity to miss an opportunity.

For example, shame on this rabbi: Even before Pope Benedict XVI's scheduled 2009 visit to Israel, the resident rabbi of Jerusalem's Western Wall preemptively announced that it was not proper for the Pontiff to arrive at the site wearing a cross. This in spite of what the Talmud says, "Righteous people of all nations have a share in the world to come."

The Jews are a wandering people of mixed cultures and diverse practices; they should know better than to denigrate any other people or their symbols. They don't all come from Poland or New York. It was a Yemenite sage, Nethanel ben al-Fayyumi, who better anticipated a papal visit to Judaism's holiest shrine when he declared in the twelfth century: "God sends a prophet to every people according to their own language."

Just as Jewish prelates routinely come to visit Christian sites wearing yarmulkes (skullcaps) if they choose, the leader of the Roman Catholic Church can hardly be instructed to remove his crucifix when visiting the Western Wall in Jerusalem. It is exactly because this is Judaism's most divine site that such an outrageous and patronizing claim should not only be withheld, but also panned.

To make matters worse, this resident rabbi (who, incidentally, speaks for Orthodox Jews only, and thereby also excludes women as full participants in Jewish liturgy) made his demand based on the myopic claim that the cross is a symbol that causes Jews distress and fear. The world will be a better place when folks stop dipping history in blood and realize, for example, that the Christian cross is a sign of peace. Even if some Christians haven't upheld that over the centuries, it doesn't change the truth.

When I have twice been a guest of the Vatican in private visits to the Sistine Chapel, nobody asked me to remove the Star of David I wear around my neck. And I am no official of the synagogue community. The papacy represents a central, global church and the Pope always wears the cross as part of his normal and official regalia. I wonder if this rabbi of the Western Wall has forgotten the message of the Torah tradition: "He who welcomes his fellow-man is as one who welcomes the Divine Presence"?

I recall that upon inheriting the senior rabbinic position at a major congregation in California, two of the fine, hard-working secretaries came to me and requested my permission to resume wearing their crucifix necklaces while at work. I was completely dumbfounded: "Why aren't you wearing them now?" Because, they nervously told me, my predecessor had instructed that it was inappropriate for them to do so in a Jewish institution. I sent the nice ladies home for the day and told them to come back tomorrow wearing whatever they wanted that connected them to God. I have never stopped being mortified by what they had to ask me.

I cherish a photo given to me by a friend: Pope John Paul II is praying at the Western Wall in 2000, stuffing a written prayer between the cracks, just as Jews have done for centuries. The snapshot clearly shows him wearing a golden cross while praying. Clearly, what we had there was heavenly. Perhaps my fundamentalist and decidedly inhospitable colleagues in Jerusalem have walked into the Wall too many times. When we have the leader of one billion Catholics honoring Jewish holy ground only sixty years after the Holocaust, then what we have is an agreement.

A SPIRITUAL APPROACH, ONE that embraces the universalism of human yearning, softens the lines and brings down the walls. It allows us to make a bed with scripture—a literature ironically filled with revealing inconsistencies and useful nuances. It may indeed be divine words, but it is not "God's Word." If it were, how does one explain the contradictions rampant within it?

Let's start with the Creation story. There are two versions of it in the Bible. They appear successively in chapters 1 and 2 of Genesis. One would think a book penned by the Creator/God would be consistent at the gate with Creation.

Like many others, I grew up with the understanding that human beings were created last in the Genesis story, namely on the sixth and final day of God's creative activity. In the first chapter of the book, we see the following verse:

> *And God made the beast of the earth after his kind, and cattle after their kind, and everything that creepeth upon the earth after his kind: and God saw that it was good. And God said, Let us make man in our image, after our likeness: and let them have dominion over the fish of the sea, and over the fowl of the air, and over the cattle, and over all the earth, and over every creeping thing that*

creepeth upon the earth. So God created man in his own image, in the image of God created he him; male and female created he them.

It's pretty evident here that the animals were created before Adam and Eve. But now take a look at the following verse, which appears in the second chapter—just a few paragraphs later:

And God said, It is not good that the man should be alone; I will make him a help meet for him. And out of the ground the LORD God formed every beast of the field, and every fowl of the air; and brought them unto Adam to see what he would call them: and whatsoever Adam called every living creature, that was the name thereof.

So in this second telling, within the same book, "the man" is already around and then God makes the animals and presents them to Adam for naming and designation. The scripture was canonized with this—and countless other irregularities—and this is clearly a problem for fundamentalists and zealots who demand God as the author.

But this is not a hindrance for people of the spirit, who celebrate the divine literature as lyrical material written by men and women inspired by God. Perhaps what matters is not the sequence—that is, which appeared first, people or beasts? Maybe what really matters is how human beings and other creatures coexist on this planet, how we refrain from wantonly slaughtering birds and other wildlife, and how we judiciously regulate the merciful killing of animals in order to help feed a postmodern world ravaged by hunger and environmental upheaval that threatens a fair distribution of food around the globe.

There are endless discrepancies in scripture, which make it a document in sync with the flaws of life and congruent with human experience. Again, the Creation paradox: In the first chapter, Adam and Eve are created simultaneously.

> *So God created man in his own image, in the image of God created he him; male and female created he them.*

However, in the second chapter, again just a few columns down, we have a completely different sequence, as well as the origin of the famous "Adam's rib," which is totally missing in chapter 1:

> *And the LORD God caused a deep sleep to fall upon Adam, and he slept: and he took one of his ribs, and closed up the flesh instead thereof; And the rib, which the LORD God had taken from man, made he a woman, and brought her unto the man.*

This simply isn't the same writer, and he or she certainly isn't someone or something that is perfect. But life isn't perfect, nor is art. Hardly impeccable are the yearnings and reveries of men, women, and children. We venerate Shakespeare and Dickens and Balzac and Mark Twain exactly because they give us realism and rawness more than they offer us chronologies and bliss.

What matters more—the numerical order in which people first appeared on Earth or the good order we human beings repeatedly fail to achieve on Earth? When you are in spiritual sorrow about your marriage or your child hurts you, do you reference someone's rib or are you mulling over your broken heart?

Beyond that, when it comes to how the world came about, why the literal obsession with the Six Days of Creation? You can believe the world evolved in six divisions, but why impose a twenty-four-hour per day clock on an enchanted story that gives a clearly scientific process the warm embellishments of hope, creativity, and light? Day One may have been the clock equivalent of three million years; Day Four might have been the Ice Age; Day Six, the interlude of cave dwellers. Why lock God into an iPhone timer? Aren't we already too much the slaves of time management?

Religion and science are not incompatible; in fact, they require each other. Even Albert Einstein, arguably the greatest scientist of all time, conceded there was some kind of divine spark that preceded everything rational. I believe religion is science with love and spirituality is hope without math.

The very opening of the Bible is a plea for imagination. Here is a beautiful sentence, one filled with music and possibility: "And God said, 'Let there be light.' And there was light."

It's interesting that the pronouncement of "light" comes immediately. However, the account of the formation of "the lights" does not appear until the fourth day—well down a few verses:

And God made two great lights; the greater light to rule the day, and the lesser light to rule the night.

So if the sun and the moon were not created till the fourth day, what exactly was this "light" that is revealed at the very outset? Besides the textual inconsistency also apparent here, what is going on? How do the literalists rationalize this?

They do so by explaining it spiritually. For the Jews, the light is not a galactic body, but heavenly wisdom revealing itself for human enlightenment. For Christians, it is the first manifestation of Christ. For example, the Mormons teach, "The Light of Christ is the divine energy, power, or influence that proceeds from God through Christ and gives life and light to all things." In other words, we are not talking about the sun at the get-go. We are talking about the creative power that governs all bodies and all beings. This is what Native Americans reverently call "The Great Spirit." Even people who are rationally based acknowledge there is something "other-like" about the first mention of light in this story. I've heard physicists express the notion that this first light was perhaps a concentrated, diffused glow, using the free hydrogen in space. So before the science, before the solar, there was the spiritual.

Old Jewish sources dig deep in their mystical exploration of this wondrous inconsistency at the start of scripture. They actually revel in the mystery and discrepancy, placing it into the category of heavenly secrets.

These texts describe the light created at the outset as something that is simply not part of our present-day natural reality. "The light which God created on the first day," says the Talmud's Rabbi Elazar, "A man could see with it from one end of the world to the other."

Another voice from the rabbis: "It (the Light) cannot shine by day. It is not the sun. It would dim the sun. It cannot shine at night—for it was created only for that very moment. So where is it? It was hidden. It is preserved for the righteous in the World to Come."

"Where did He hide it?" asks the Zohar, the book of Kabbalistic intrigue. The answer: "In the Torah." None of these sages, men who the fundamentalists quote freely, were stuck on literalism. They were visionaries and romanticists. They were the kind of people Robert F. Kennedy, a Catholic, was thinking about when he paraphrased George Bernard Shaw and declared: "Some men see things as they are and say why. I dream things that never were and say why not."

Now this is a theology that works for me because it isn't prose; it is poetry. And what makes it lyrical is the very contradiction between the light of Creation and the light of the sun.

Remember the story of Moses arguing with God at the crest of Mt. Sinai because the Hebrews below had distrustfully constructed the

Golden Calf? Moses's willingness to take on God is crucial. It is a critical moment when a human being works out of the liturgical box and quells the deity's anger-management problems. But it also happens to be a chronological glitch for people who insist the Bible was written by God.

The Sinai clash between Moses and God is found in chapter 32 of Exodus. Moses is up there receiving the Ten Commandments. The problem is that the Ten Commandments were already unveiled in chapter 20 of Exodus. Twelve full chapters of depictions and enactments have unfolded between these two sections. In chapter 24, Moses is running around among the people, describing and interpreting his adventures on the mount, dispatching young men to offer celebratory burnt offerings. In chapter 26, architects and weavers are designing the portable tabernacle for the tablets of laws. In chapter 27, Moses and his brother Aaron are gathering "pure olive oil" for the original "Eternal Lamp" of the tabernacle—now reenacted in every synagogue as the so-called *Ner Tamid* (Eternal Light) above the ark that contains the Torah scrolls. In chapter 28, the high priests are busy designing their vestments and choosing linen colors. In chapter 30, Moses and his staff are taking a preliminary census of the people and assessing a basic tax for each individual. A lot has happened since Moses went up the peak and came back down with the law.

Now we're in chapter 32 and, lo and behold, Moses is back at the top and taking the heat for the people's collective sin of idolatry down on the ground. Completely out of chronology, without any explanation, we find the following verse that opens this episode:

And when the people saw that Moses delayed to come down out of the mount, the people gathered themselves unto Aaron and said unto him: "Up, make us a god, which shall go before us; as for this

Moses, the man that brought us out of Egypt, we don't know what has become of him.

What unfolds here is the hysteria and panic that led to the blasphemous assembly of the Golden Calf and that converted the pastoral interlude between Moses and God upstairs into a dangerous exchange of threats and rebuttals. It is a tense little drama and, again, it emboldens human beings to argue with fate when there is a moral imperative to do so. But in terms of the flow of the book, it's a major sequential error. How could this possibly happen if the tome was written by the Almighty God?

Ronald L. Conte Jr., a Roman Catholic theologian and Bible translator, has stated it simply: "In Biblical chronology, there is usually a substantial possibility of error." Indeed. It is actually refreshing that a thoughtful, self-proclaimed "disciple of Christ" like Conte is so open about the many gaping textual holes in the scripture.

The Jewish tradition slides into rationalization when it comes to this vexing problem, such as appears between Exodus, chapters 20 and 32. Or about the fact that there are two versions of the Creation story. The ancient rabbis opined, with genuine concern, I am sure: "There is no early or late in the Bible." In other words, God has his own clock and whatever happens in the text—even if it doesn't click time-wise—is just the way it is.

And yet, the stern clerics require that we literally follow an exacting calibration of numerals, times, intervals, locations, calendars, indexes, manuals, cycles, dress codes, hair styles, menstrual patterns, migrations, and milestone procedurals to the letter and by the clock or we are out of the game. This tyranny is manifest in every religious denomination, and it is lightened or adjusted only when the scripture throws an anomaly at the presiding officers. For example, when the scholars encountered the abnormality of Moses being at the summit of Mt. Sinai within two contradictory moments in Exodus, these scholars became, well, very *spiritual* in their interpretation of time.

Meanwhile, exactly to whom did a prominent angel speak when it came to prophesying the birth of Christ? Which earthly parent, Mary or Joseph? It depends upon where you look in the New Testament, specifically, which of the Gospels you examine.

In the Gospel according to Matthew, the angel notifies the human father, Joseph:

> *An angel of the Lord appeared to him in a dream and said, "Joseph, son of David, do not be afraid to take Mary home as your wife, because what is conceived in her is from the Holy Spirit."*

It's a different story in the Gospel according to Luke:

> *God sent the angel Gabriel to Nazareth, a town in Galilee, to a virgin pledged to be married to a man named Joseph, a descendant of David. The virgin's name was Mary. The angel went to her and said, "Greetings, you who are highly favored! The Lord is with you."*

Here the angel has a name and there are specific geographic references. Mary, who is only here identified as a virgin, is the one being addressed. In fact, among the Four Gospels, the very birth of Christ is referenced in merely these two volumes. This astonishing detail has never been reconciled in the organized Christian community or even the fact that according to Matthew, the Davidic genealogy of Jesus is superimposed (without any textual evidence) on the father, Joseph. However, by Luke, the messianic lineage comes directly through Mary and her virginity. The angel goes straight to her and announces that she is "favored" and that God is with her.

In his 1995 survey, New Testament Contradictions, the religious philosopher Paul Carlson states flatly:

"Of all the writers of the New Testament, only Matthew and Luke mention the virgin birth. Had something as miraculous as the virgin birth actually occurred, one would expect that Mark and John would have at least mentioned it in their efforts to convince the world that Jesus was who they were claiming him to be. The apostle Paul never mentions the virgin birth, even though it would have strengthened his arguments in several places."

I don't mention this startling inconsistency to disprove or discredit anything or anyone. On the contrary: It is illuminating and reassuring to me that the New Testament is distilled by human storytelling rather than inviolate when it comes to absolute veracity. Nobody who was ever helped by his or her relationship with Jesus—who saw light in a dark place or was motivated to feed somebody who was hungry—first stopped and scrutinized the literary problems of the collective Gospels. That person was moved by the tenderness of Jesus, not by his birth records. An old collection of data that doesn't all fall into place on the page doesn't affect the future unless we get wedged in it.

Most of us do not have all the facts when it comes to the genealogies of our own parents and grandparents. But since when did that suddenly skew how real they are or were for us, how they touched us, lifted, sometimes angered us, but ultimately shaped us? I'm not really certain about what my departed father did when he was a child, who he hung out with, what he believed as a young man, and I certainly do not have (nor want) any details about his conception. But I surely remember what my soul felt like the day he first took me to a professional baseball game, how the ballpark frank tasted on my lips, how he smiled and cheered and touched my hair that day. My love for him is not legislated; it is (to paraphrase the Lebanese poet Kahlil Gibran) life's longing for itself.

Don't get stuck on scriptural literalism; it's got less to do with the way life works than how a healthy mix of faith and spirituality enable you to believe in this human experience and to deal with its ambiguities. The Bible may be a tool, but it is not a hammer. Even Paul, the sainted founder of Christianity, a Jew who had an epiphany on the road to Damascus and blessed the world with the benevolent potential of Christ, once declared: "What business is it of mine to judge those outside the church? Are you not to judge those inside?" In other words, Paul was not about evaluating you; he was more about holding "the insiders" to an ethical standard.

Mohammed also never espoused the exclusivity of any tradition or any singular religious code. Known as "The Prophet," he declared: "The people of God say: 'There are as many ways to God as the breaths of the creatures' and every breath emanates from the heart according to the belief the heart has of God." Spiritual inclusiveness is clearly embedded in the Holy Quran—even if some radical Muslims have lost touch with their own divination in this troubling twenty-first century: "Wherever you turn, there is the face of God." Nobody has the last word on your spirit.

And that is exactly what I was thinking one day in Jerusalem, several years ago. Jerusalem—city of Teddy Kollek, *kaffiyeh*-laden Arab merchants, Jewish worshippers, and Christian soothsayers—the tormented village where Jesus spoke the Hebrew Psalms during his darkest hour on Calvary.

I stood by the Western Wall, the 187-foot long, last retaining flank of the biblical Holy Temple, godliest Jewish site on Earth, and the place where people come in tears and song and dance and insert their scrawled notes of supplication into the cracks between the stones. Like everybody else on the plaza that sweeps down to the old wall of rock, moss, and wailing, I know this is a place like no other on Earth.

Jerusalem, a dream in painful progress, torn from inside, with imperial war stains practically still visible across crescent domes and ringing Christian bells and swift taxis and beleaguered mules—the ultimate paradox of Semitic spirituality and secularism. This person over here is covered in black, Polish-origin robes and a fur-lined religious hat; that one over there hurries down in Israeli military garb, Uzi machine gun strapped on his shoulder as he is texting his girlfriend on his smartphone. Here on the plaza, with its protective Hasidic clans, as thick as blackberries, the Arab-dominated Damascus Gate only a sprint away, men and women tensely comingle in the largest open-air revival marketplace anywhere.

I stood at the Wall, implanted my written devotion into a gap between two of the golden stones, and closed my eyes. I do like and honor prayer books but did not need one at that moment on God's arcade. I heard the cadenced chant of a religious fellow near me. I knew the entreaties he whispered in a perfunctory fashion under his breath because of my upbringing and experience. My eyes opened and I noticed that as he swayed, he turned the pages of his worn, small Hebrew prayer book dutifully but he did not particularly look at the pages. He was functional in his discharge of the late afternoon liturgy as the sun hung low on the horizon. The robed gentleman, with side locks and high black hat, was to my right. He was a "Hasid"—a member of the numinous sect founded in Poland in the eighteenth century and unforgiving toward ritual leniency.

To my left was a chubby, middle-aged man, apparently Jewish, clearly American, not garlanded in theological apparel—a borrowed, paper skullcap positioned awkwardly on his head. He was wearing a quiet, pinstriped suit and suitably matching tie. He looked at me and said, quietly, "My first time here." I smiled at him and noticed his eyes were filled with tears. He had no book; both of his stubby hands were now placed on the citadel. His round shoulders shook and he leaned his head against the wall, sobbing and succumbing and releasing some ineffable burden he brought to this sanctified site.

Now he murmured something indistinguishable from deep within himself just as the Hasid closed his tiny book, exhaled a mechanical "Amen," and walked briskly behind me. He noticed the secular novice and scowled at both him and me. I turned to my left and thought I saw an angelic light rising to the stars now glowing above the Holy City. Who are we mortals to judge one another when it comes to the soul?

Chapter Six

BETTER THAN THE MIRACLES

I THINK A LOT about a distressed woman in the Bible who has no name, no known community, and not much hope. She is described in the Book of Deuteronomy as "a captive lady"—she is a prisoner of war. Her legs are chained, her wrists are bleeding from tight ropes cutting into her skin, and her eyes are bulging with terror. The implication is that she is attractive; her predicament is treacherous and quite possibly fatal. The same Bible that began with light and creation often dwells heavily on the particulars and regulations of war, conquest, and dominion. People sometimes have a hard time with its unforgiving tone in these matters.

When you read the Book of Joshua, for example, you are reading a military commander's genocidal manual: His Hebrew army is commanded to do nothing less than to completely slaughter and expunge the indigenous peoples of Canaan because the Hebrew God, Yahweh, has chosen to give the land to them. It's not easy to study this material without shaking your head a bit in disillusionment and skepticism.

At one point in this volume, God wondrously holds the sun in place so that Joshua would have ample time in daylight to finish off the Amorites—one of the Canaanite populations. I don't ponder the miracle; however, I reflect on the massacre.

But here, in Deuteronomy, the war drums are gratifyingly muffled. The grisly narrative is interrupted with a surprisingly touching intervention on behalf of that female POW. At exactly the moment of her total helplessness, when the hearts of crazed male soldiers are pounding with suppression and lust, when they have been seduced by their own fears and their cosmic machismo, the Bible reaches out to protect this woman. And it is also saving these dangerously feverish soldiers from their own worst instincts.

The Hebrew soldiers are instructed not to mistreat the prisoner, and they are charged to let her restore her vanity and dignity:

> When you go to war against your enemies and the Lord your God delivers them into your hands and you take captives, if you notice among the captives a beautiful woman and are attracted to her, you may take her as your wife. Bring her into your home and have her shave her head, trim her nails and put aside the clothes she was wearing when captured. After she has lived in your house and mourned her father and mother for a full month, then you may go to her and be her husband and she shall be your wife. If you are not pleased with her, let her go. You must not sell her or treat her as a slave, since you have dishonored her.

In other words, don't think of your female captive as an object. Let her clean up, and hand her some fresh clothing. Let her grieve for her lost home. And if you want to have sex with her, you have to marry her. And then if you realize she isn't for you, do not throw her into the trash of battle. Let her go home to her family. Be a real man.

This is astonishingly progressive stuff that was written over three thousand years ago. It certainly is not found in today's military literature.

An irony: Hardly anybody knows about this little flash of sanity and compassion in the Bible, including the ones who routinely employ it to evangelize and dominate other people. It is not the account of an official "miracle." Yet is it not miraculous? Doesn't it touch your heart more than yet another parting sea that drowns Egyptians or a thundering mountain that wreaks lethal havoc on Hebrews?

Then there is the tale of the prophet-for-hire and his talking donkey.

In the Book of Numbers, a guileful, professional diviner named Balaam is introduced at about the time the former Hebrew slaves are nearing the Promised Land. A regional desert king named Balak is highly agitated about the Hebrews: They are about to cut across his territory and he has heard about their improbable escape from Egypt and about their deity that routinely brutalizes anybody who gets in the Hebrews' way. Balak decides it's time to get somebody credentialed in spells to curse the Hebrews and their leader, Moses. He hires Balaam, who is highly prized as a roving seer with a donkey and who knows all the proper enchantments.

After a couple of false starts, Balaam gets going and finds a high place from which to professionally blaspheme the Hebrews and rid Balak of them. En route, his donkey temporarily becomes a stumbling block. The animal abruptly stops and refuses to move forward. But not only that—suddenly, the donkey attains the power of human speech and complains that Balaam is abusing him. The animal declares: "Am I not your own donkey, which you have always ridden, to this day? Have I been in the habit of doing this to you?"

Balaam has no patience for this: "You have made a fool of me! If only I had a sword in my hand, I would kill you right now." Luckily, for both man and beast, "an angel" is seen along the mountain path and the journey is resumed. Again I choose to lose this little phenomenon, a talking ass and a convenient peacemaking seraph, in favor of what happens afterward inside Balaam's heart.

Balaam, now with the thankfully mute donkey, makes his way up to a high point above the desert. The Bible tells us this less-than-noble opportunist beholds the Hebrews down below and in the distance. He makes them out, their masses and their livestock and their tents, in the blistering sunny haze. He squints and clears his throat. He walks around the shrubs and pauses under a patch of date palms. Let me see, what kind of terrible curse can I lay on these people?

Now he thinks about the several pieces of silver he will earn from the nervous King Balak for this procedure. He likely assumes the merciless desert will consume this wandering, stateless throng of ex-slaves anyway; this job is a sure winner and he again will be venerated as an omniscient seer. This will be especially beneficial for his curriculum vitae.

Then something happens. The cunning old soothsayer is stirred by a burst of beneficence and goodwill. God gets into his heart. The Bible says:

> When Balaam saw that it pleased the LORD to bless Israel, he did not go, as at other times, to look for omens, but set his face toward the wilderness. And Balaam lifted up his eyes and saw Israel camping tribe by tribe.

Again, it doesn't matter where you are when you feel your spirit moved. And you don't have to be a Jew, a Christian, or a Muslim—Balaam was a pagan. Rather than cursing the Hebrews, and in spite of his coming paycheck, Balaam bursts into a rather famous set of lyrics:

> The oracle of Balaam the son of Beor,
> The oracle of the man whose eye is opened,
> The oracle of him who hears the words of God,

Who sees the vision of the Almighty,
Falling down with his eyes uncovered:
How lovely are your tents, O Jacob,
Your dwelling-places, O Israel!

That closing phrase, "How lovely are your tents, O Jacob, Your dwelling places, O Israel!" has for centuries been, in its original Hebrew, the best-known and most often recited morning chant in the Jewish prayer book. Very few Jews even know that its origin was from the mouth of an amoral, un-churched, practiced mystic who saw something in the Hebrews that overruled his unscrupulousness.

So I know the donkey spoke to Balaam in this tale, and I understand the text inserts an interceding angel to clear the way for Balaam becoming a man "whose eye is opened." But the supernatural stuff, while colorful, is not what holds my interest, and you don't need to believe in it to make this story meaningful for you.

What this story tells me is that we remain biased against another people or another culture—and we are even prepared to excoriate them—until we have the chance to actually see and get to know them. The humanization of our neighbors is more important than the deification of our gods. The spiritual triumph here is that Balaam had no critical interest in or understanding of the Jewish people below until he opened his eyes and saw them, heard their songs from the distance, noticed their children running about, saw grandparents hugging their little ones, observed men and women interacting, seeking shade, drawing water from their dug wells.

It's not about a chattering mule. It's about the fact that human bias can be mitigated by real contact with "the other." When we come to know folks from another creed, we begin to humanize them. And their dwelling places become lovely and their tents are no longer ghettoized from our moral field of vision.

Many years ago, I faced a tense moment in front of the board of a prominent and historic temple I served in Ohio. A new, unadorned congregation of Jewish gays and lesbians had been meeting in a space rented from a local church. They were coming upon their first anniversary as a synagogue and wanted to commemorate the milestone in our sanctuary. A leasing contract would be required. There was resistance to this on the part of some of the trustees. A few of the comments made in an initial meeting were repugnant: "Homosexuality is forbidden in the Torah!" (This is contradicted by the David and Jonathan story, as we have seen.) One person said flatly, "I don't want this temple to be associated with those kinds of people."

I personally knew the leader of the gay congregation. He was an articulate, pensive, and reverent man. The board agreed to let me present him at the subsequent session to make his case directly. At least if they'd see him and listen to him, perhaps their biases would melt into humanization. It was all I could do to contain my own rage at the hypocrisy of the reaction of the board at the outset: They were quite selective when quoting the Torah for their bursts of moral outrage. They did not keep kosher. They drove their automobiles on the Sabbath. Several members of the temple's professional choir were gay and lesbian musicians. Beyond that, I was well aware of homosexual situations within some of their families but remained circumspect.

Sid joined me at the next meeting. I didn't try to manage what he would say out of respect for his intelligence and sincerity. But I could not have guessed what Sid would come up with to move and humble the adversarial elements of the committee. He was asked, "Why should we let you lease space from us?"

Sid folded his hands. He was not intimidated. He spoke in that kind of audible whisper that has more power than shouting.

"I know all of you do this volunteer work because you love the Torah. Your congregation reads and studies the weekly portion in the correct cycle. Our congregation does the same. We have one old and worn Torah scroll compared to the several you have but it's all the same tradition and the same calendar of readings."

"What's your point?" One of the trustees clearly had no patience, let alone tolerance. Sid nodded but was undaunted.

"I'd like to refer you to a favorite incident of mine that we read every year," he said.

Where was Sid going with this? I thought.

"It's a pretty important moment in the text. This fellow who does prophecies for a living is told to curse the Hebrews in the desert by a king who is anxious about them. He fears them for some reason. The king doesn't know them or anything about them so he feels threatened. The prophet he hires is named Balaam."

Again an interruption from the inhospitable trustee: "Hey, that's the guy with the talking ass!"

The group unexpectedly bellowed with laughter. A faint smile formed on Sid's face.

"Yes," he said, quietly. "The talking ass." The laughter faded as Sid now was drawing the trustees in.

He continued, "But it's not the donkey that stands out for me. I didn't come here to share that part of the story with you. It's what happens when Balaam finally gets up to curse the Hebrews. I'm sure you all know what actually occurred. He didn't curse them because he got close enough to see them. He wound up blessing them. They weren't strangers anymore because he let himself get to know them. He got beyond his face-value judgments about them. He even gave up the silver the king had given him to curse them. He actually sang their praises."

I couldn't contain myself. I was so proud of Sid and also proud of my trustees. They were moved. Setting caution aside, I began to chant the Hebrew prayer that all of them knew even as it would now have a new meaning for them. The whole room sang:

> *Ma tovu ohalekha Ya'akov, mishk'notekha Yisra'el.* ("How goodly are your tents, O Jacob, Your dwelling places, O Israel.")

The Board of Trustees voted unanimously to offer space to Sid's congregation—at no cost. As Sid and I walked out together he looked at me and then exclaimed, "Now that was a miracle!"

THE TERM, MIRACLE, IS exploited, overworked, and inflated. It is also dangerous because religious prelates use it as a cynical tool to manipulate people into obeisance. Whether it is right-wing Christian groups garnering thousands upon thousands of dollars by promising people "the glory of afterlife," Muslim caliphs brainwashing youngsters into becoming suicide bombers, or fanatic Jewish authorities terrorizing Palestinian villages "in the name of Torah," it is shameful. We need to be cautious with extreme religious righteousness, or we will simply divine one another into oblivion.

I remember when, just after Israel's stunning victory in the Six Day War in June of 1967, the kind Orthodox rabbi of our family's synagogue stood up on the pulpit before the Sabbath morning congregation. I loved Rabbi Indich and bless his memory. He was sincerely engaged in a mystical relationship with God and scripture. He was a fundamentalist nonetheless; there were no nuances in the text, no human lyricism, no deviation from what God had written down for all times. Every cataclysm, from the parting of the Red Sea to the sun standing still for Joshua to complete his warfare, was an original and inviolate act of heaven. That's how the gentle man made some sense out of a world that rarely made sense.

On that particular morning, his red beard shining in the sunlight that came protracted through stained glass windows, his voluminous prayer shawl and its fringes dancing on his tall frame as he shook his arms in fervency, his bluish eyes brimming with tears and devotion, the rabbi unabashedly declared: "What just now happened in *Eretz Yisroel* (The Land of Israel) is nothing short of a bona fide miracle—equal to any miracle we find in the Torah!"

Indeed, there was the sense that what transpired in the Middle East, the astoundingly bold and successful surprise attack by Israel against the amassed armies of several Arab nations on its borders, all of which had been publicly committed to "kill all the Jews or drown them in the Mediterranean Sea," was miraculous. After all, the world had written off the tiny Jewish state's possibility of surviving the onslaught and a number of rabbis had traveled up and down the countryside sanctifying lands as new burial sites for the expected accumulation of dead Jews.

But I'm not so sure it was an actual miracle. Eight hundred young Israeli soldiers had died in battle, as well as countless thousands of Arab youngsters who had been conscripted into their national armed forces. I suspected even then the Israeli military command, dealing with an unprecedented existential threat, was more infatuated with their meticulous armament-based calibrations and the bravery of their militias and airmen, with the endless drills and cunning leadership that sparked the triumph than they were with the intervention of angels.

The city of Jerusalem, divided for the previous nineteen years by the outcome of the 1948 Independence War in which my father fought, was indeed reunited for Teddy Kollek to try to govern with wisdom. The reunification of the Holy City was the epicenter of messianic associations that many Jews—and Christians—asserted with the startling outcome of the 1967 conflict.

But when I walked through the still battle-beaten, stony streets of eastern Jerusalem during a visit just a few weeks after the war, I saw several blood-stained mounds of rocks and inscribed prayers and heart-rending mementos left behind where Israeli soldiers had fallen during the brutish hand-to-hand fighting with Jordanian troops. A lot of horrors were experienced along the way to the Wailing Wall, which the Israelis recaptured and which Israeli zealots then beatified as God's will. A verifiable apocalyptic event would have been much cleaner, I submit. And it would have been void of all the gashing, the bullets, the bombs, the tortured endings, and then the whitewashing politics that made this monumental turning point less of a miracle and more of a costly and brilliant victory for the side that was so flagrantly threatened by extermination.

Meanwhile, the legacy of Rabbi Indich's "miracle" is hardly miraculous. Nearly fifty years later, Israel is still beleaguered, the Arab nations are in the throes of upheaval and terror, while Jerusalem's Palestinian babies are getting very little fresh milk from either side. Neither Yahweh nor Allah has been particularly wondrous in the category of inspiration. Both the Torah and Quran have been exploited shamelessly by radical men who need to give way to the inspiration of genuine human creativity.

Now that would be a miracle.

Better we should believe in the small moments that are found in the old texts. You can believe in the scripture when it reads like your own life, not as the diary of saints and archangels. I'm at home with the religious Bible when I read about the manner in which the young Jacob loved Rachel. In Genesis, the same book that sends me a flood to drown in, I am much more affected by the young man's gushing tears. Describing the moment when Jacob beheld the woman of his dreams, the text simply declares: "And Jacob wept." I've seen that; *I've felt that.*

When Jacob has to flee his parents' home because of the dangerous trouble he had with his twin brother Esau, he winds up utterly alone in the squid ink-darkness of the desert. Sibling rivalries have sent me to the same place; no doubt you as well. There comes a time when family dysfunction thrusts every one of us into a wilderness of despair and heartache. We are beyond the reach of our own parents who have either abandoned us in some way or have simply died.

The loneliness of such times is crippling, and we often feel recovery is beyond our reach. We may certainly pray and there is therapy in that. But we know relief is ultimately found within ourselves. This is not about a miracle but about an inner revelation and that is why you and I have been there.

That is what Jacob discovered during this same interlude—a teenager alone in the darkness, divided emotionally and geographically from his family. The young man laid himself to sleep under the stars, using a rock for a pillow, and trembled into a fitful slumber. He dreamed a dream: a ladder extended from the heavens to Earth. Angels were descending and ascending this wondrous staircase. Hope filled up in Jacob's soul as he awoke, suddenly uplifted and unafraid. There was no one else around but the boy spoke out: "God was in this place but I, I did not know it!"

I've seen that; I've felt that. I have perceived something greater than myself exactly when I was depleted to something much less than myself. I had to—and so did you when it happened in your life. When I was fired, when I was insulted, when I divorced, when I failed, when I considered suicide—there were no miracles. There was just an intuition, a dream, a flash of hope, a memory. Something stirred me to redemption, just as something intervened in young Jacob's psyche exactly when he was at his lowest.

It may have been God at work; it may have been miraculous. But to say it was a miracle is to repudiate my own efforts, my own strength, or my own will to live. To say God did it all is to suggest that I am nothing but an empty vessel or some kind of feckless organism. It implies that I lack a brain and a heart, and that curiosity and inquisitiveness do not flow in my bloodstream. Yet every organized tradition asserts I was created in God's image. So I must have some value, and responsibility, under the sun.

When we partner with God via prayer rather than just wait for God via phenomena, then life becomes immune to the extremists who have lost their capacity to dream.

Perhaps no one in American history believed more in the human spirit than Thomas Jefferson, the third president, and effectively the author of the Declaration of Independence. For Jefferson and his comrades, the ideals of democracy and freedom were as sacrosanct as any religion. To deride Jefferson, a Founding Father of the United States, could only be classified as "un-American." Yet few men or women were ever more skeptical about biblical miracles than was Jefferson—even while he discovered a fountain of wisdom in the biblical quest for human dignity and renewal.

Jefferson was three years from his death when, in 1823, he made clear his suspicions and concerns about religious fundamentalism. He wrote: "The day will come when the mystical generation of Jesus by the Supreme Being as his father, in the womb of a virgin, will be classed with the fable of the generation of Minerva in the brain of Jupiter."

When Jefferson opened his Bible and read about the childbearing Rebekah, he likely recognized her physical and psychological anguish. Rebekah moaned as she carried the warring twins, Jacob and Esau. The text describes her pain and bewilderment while these antagonistic beings literally struggled within her womb. "If this is what it is, then I don't want to be here," she cried out to God.

Though this is a dark moment, it is the Bible at its most accessible: *Then I don't want to be here.*

What are these but suicidal feelings? Every one of us has felt this despair and hopelessness from time to time. People we loved have tragically acted on these impulses. I remember Rebekah losing her faith in life much better than I recall those twin fetuses somehow, inexplicably, dramatizing the future Middle East conflict inside her belly. I also remember well that this woman was the first person—in the entire biblical literature—who uttered a spontaneous, guttural plea to God.

No, it's not the miracles that make the Bible real for us; it's us making the Bible realistic. And the path to that is not via exploding peaks and bloody rivers and cruel gods. The path to spiritual peace is through the spirit itself, through the bittersweet wisdom of small triumphs, private revelations, and even through the therapy of grief.

I don't agree with Thomas Jefferson that someday the birth of Jesus will be totally relegated to a fable. Nor is that my hope. But I do feel what's crucial for us is not how Jesus was born. It's how he lived. And what he taught in the course of his brief, landmark time on Earth. It was Jesus who so brilliantly declawed the tyranny of the old Hebrew dietary laws and in the same breath empowered human beings to free one another. He did this when he stated, simply, in Matthew: "Not that which goes into the mouth makes a man unclean, but that which comes out of the mouth." In other words, it's not about what you eat with your mouth; it's about what you say with it, what set of beliefs and ethics you discuss and fulfill.

I once saw a real miracle happening before my eyes. It was called "the blessing of the hands." It involved no fanfare, no accolades expressed from a pulpit, and no vanities published in a church bulletin. In fact, no one is expected to even know this little miracle is ongoing: It takes place in the well-hidden basement laundry of a Catholic children's hospital.

The physicians operate on children with cancer, congenital heart problems, cystic fibrosis, and myriad other dreadful conditions that have flanked childhood. It's to them that we anoint the well-deserved credit for so often saving young lives. But the quiet workers down below deliver instruments free of bacteria. Accordingly, an aged but vibrant Sister of Mercy blesses their hands before they soak, steam, and purify. That's it— no media coverage, no drama, no frills. The woman blesses their hands. They look forward to it and when asked, one of them explained to me, "We don't need anybody to know. We just need to have our hands blessed so the knives will be clean and the children will live."

Who could see such a thing in such a place and not know there is a God?

Chapter Seven

THE REAL PEOPLE IN SCRIPTURE WERE SPIRITUAL PRAGMATISTS

"Up, make us a God!"
—THE HEBREWS TO AARON, EXODUS 32

IT'S NOT ALWAYS EASY being the sibling of a superstar. This is especially true when you are the older brother of a legendary man. Such was the plight of Aaron, a character in scripture who performed no miracles, watched in horror as his two sons were burned alive by heaven for offering an inappropriate ritual, and generally covered for his brother Moses when the leader needed an alibi or some shielding from criticism.

We shall see through these instances that Aaron, the anointed leader of the desert priests, was ultimately a realist and a spiritual pragmatist. He was a lot like you and me—trying to do his best and trying to have faith, often under trying and frustrating circumstances.

We have already established that we don't know why the drama of the Golden Calf, when Moses suddenly reappears at the top of Mt. Sinai (while serious chicanery is happening down below), materializes in the Bible twelve full chapters after Moses already went up Mt. Sinai to obtain the Ten Commandments. We also don't have any explanation why Moses, without breathing much of a word to anybody, abandons his post and takes off to go commiserate with the Almighty.

Perhaps this has something to do with a realistic and normal sequence in human life: From time to time, every one of us feels God is pulling us toward a purpose we didn't expect or anticipate. The prompt may be a trauma, an illness, a betrayal by a lover, or simply a moment of heartfelt revelation about what we need to do. It could be an unexpected burst of jubilation—a ballpark home run, a pay raise, or the long overdue smell of rain. When that happens, it usually evolves in a spiritual breakthrough and not while we are holding a prayer book or reciting rote liturgy in a church or temple or mosque. There is simply no indication in the Bible that Moses took off, unannounced, to visit with God while sitting in the pews of a synagogue. He simply responded to a call he heard.

What is clear, however, is that Moses left everybody hanging, so to speak, when he split the scene. We understand this because of what we read in the startling opening of chapter 32 in the Book of Exodus:

And when the people saw that Moses delayed to come down out of the mount, the people gathered themselves unto Aaron.

In other words, the helpless Aaron, stuck at ground level, is abruptly confronted with a mob. Moses is up in the clouds, enjoying karma with God. Aaron—inexplicably and unfairly—is challenged by the fallout from Moses's indiscriminate departure from his duties. Moses defaults on his visibility as the leader of a nervous, panicky, and confused throng of former slaves who need the comfort and reassurance of the man who marched them out from Pharaoh's grip in Egypt.

One can only imagine the bewilderment and consternation of those pitiful wilderness wayfarers, still looking over their shoulders for

Egyptian chariots, having only the person of Moses as a buffer against their deepest hysteria and fears, blinking into the hot horizon without the man who swore their deliverance. Could they be blamed for going after the brother who is readily accessible and, in their minds, liable? Can they be impugned for transferring their angst at Aaron in the glaring absence of his brother?

And this is exactly the kind of sizzling torment that is brought on by religious phobia. Then and now, it is treacherously hypnotic for lost and disaffected people. Don't we read about this kind of thing every day in the newspapers; aren't we horrified by it on television? This is as old as God and as new as the reemergence of today's *fatwās*.

Reading the Bible, one can almost see the terror in Aaron's eyes as the striding gang reached him. They were in no mood for explanations; they were feverish and seething with derision and insecurity:

> *Up, make us a god! For this man Moses, the man that brought us out of the land of Egypt, we know not what has become of him.*

On that last point, Aaron could probably not have agreed more. Even though he likely knew the details of Moses's lofty assignment, he had no notion what had become of his brother. The poor man was, at once, anxious about Moses and furious with him. Aaron was now at real physical risk, all because Moses had effectively abandoned his post and left Aaron desperately exposed.

So what did Aaron do in the face of this demand, "Up, make us a god!" He thought quickly on his feet and what we see in the text is the transcript of a brilliant spiritual pragmatist. He did not ask them to kneel and pray. He did not offer a homily. He told them to get some jewelry.

*And Aaron said unto them: break off the golden earrings, which
are in the ears of your wives, of your sons, and your daughters, and
bring them to me.*

How do you stop a religious riot? Sidetrack the participants to an alternate kind of mission posthaste. Aaron seems to be playing to the crowd's ventilating command, "Up, make us a god!" In fact, he was stalling them, and sending them to acquire precisely the kinds of provisions necessary to manufacture the bull idol they craved in their panic. He was trying to buy time. Maybe his exalted brother would show up while these crazies were out collecting platinum. Aaron may have been a priest, but he was no pawn.

But there was more to his calculation than just the clever diversion toward their families' precious stones. The shrewd brother was directing these mutineers to do something that was not presumably possible. Break off the earrings, which are in the ears of your wives? Right, that would go over well with the women! (Men don't readily part with their valuables, either.) It wasn't like the ladies could make such a collective sacrifice and then run over to Tiffany's to garner some replacement gems. Aaron, a man who performed rituals but thought rationally, assumed the wives would not be so hasty in handing over their brooches and baubles.

It should be noted the significant cache of bullion associated with the wandering Hebrew slaves is unabashedly identified in the Bible as war booty. The desert God had told Moses at the start of their dialogue, when first encountering the shepherd at the Burning Bush, that the Hebrews "will not leave Egypt empty-handed." The Hebrew women were instructed to take from the Egyptian women "jewels of silver, and jewels of gold, and raiment." This treasure would later be used in the building of the wilderness sanctuary. The world's original freedom march was not lacking in currency or exquisite building materials.

This dazzling truth is not widely known or discussed by the religious purists. I don't remember hearing about it in Hebrew school. It appears in the text unambiguously and unapologetically. It makes some people uncomfortable; others exploit it for cynical purposes or simply out of anti-Semitism. (In 2003, an Egyptian law professor attempted to organize a class-action lawsuit against "all Jews of the world" for plundering the assets of ancient Egypt.) As for Aaron, all he knew at the flashpoint of his scary predicament was that he had to appease the mob in order to save his neck and that he had to run the clock. The moral equation of the pillaged accessories was not on his mind. There was no time for invocations; it was time for planning. It's almost as if Aaron anticipated author Lewis Carroll's (*Alice in Wonderland*) nineteenth century rhetorical question: "Am I a deep philosopher or a great genius?"

So Aaron dispatched the people to collect the gold while betting they'd be unsuccessful. He was wrong. Here's the very next sentence in the story:

And all the peoples broke off the golden earrings, which were in their ears and brought them to Aaron.

So much for Aaron's intuition. In no time, he was overseeing a stock of hardware and not only did he cooperate (or acquiesce) to the escapade, he is said to have himself "fashioned" the idol calf out of the melted gold. In the end, he totally submitted:

And when Aaron saw it, he built an altar before it. And Aaron made a proclamation and said, tomorrow is a feast to the Lord!

Tomorrow! Aaron was still hedging. He seemed to be reasoning, hoping: "Maybe my brother will finally show up by tomorrow." Reading this account, one can envision this beleaguered, strained victim of circumstances, torn between concern for his own welfare and allegiance to his brother—even while brimming with resentment and exasperation. *This is the stuff of life;* this is what people put us through—particularly our loved ones and especially when they deny us transparency. And when they don't tell us what they are doing and thinking.

The real miracle here is that Aaron did not implode with tension and despair. I have seen corporate executives lose their cool under much less ominous conditions—someone resigns, another steals, and yet another gives away company secrets. Aaron did not take off and flee the scene. He did not quit, and he did not send the masses up the mountain after his wayward brother. He also did not fall prostrate and plead for deliverance. That is not what you do when you are facing the kind of existential threat that presented itself to this unwitting casualty of his brother's negligence.

Although his submissive actions to the mob are widely trashed and censured in the rabbinic commentary on this incident, I am on his side. What would his critics have him do? There is also a disapproving Christian treatise about him suggesting "Aaron feared the people at this moment more than he feared Yahweh."

Really? Does anyone actually believe people fear God more than they fear other people? We tremble over our demanding parents, our nagging children, our controlling bosses, and our illicit lovers who might talk. We dread looming tax collectors, white-clad physicians, and police car sirens. Before most of us even think about God on any given day, several human beings, family members, colleagues, teachers, or strangers scare us, madden us, or embroil us in their responsibilities, agendas, egos, schemes, and paranoia. So yes, Aaron was petrified of those snarling folks on the ground more than he was thinking about Yahweh up in the clouds.

In stringing along those wild-eyed, panic-stricken people while hoping Moses would rematerialize and resolve the standoff, Aaron became the quintessential spiritual pragmatist. I can believe in this basic human narrative much more than in the assertion that Moses was actually interfacing with a deity above who was, at once, carving commandments into two stones with fire while simultaneously plotting to vaporize the human beings below for whom this God was writing law.

Further down in the Old Testament, Aaron suffers an even more direct emotional tribulation. It's in Leviticus, and two of Aaron's sons are identified as priest-interns. Apparently, these two men, Nadab and Abihu, were as boisterous as they were young. They were in charge of a public sacrament involving lighting a bonfire for a certain sacrifice. The rules for the ritual were established and not to be altered. The sons made a serious miscalculation—in full view of the congregation. They each took "his censer and put fire therein, and offered a strange fire before the Lord, which he commanded them not."

The result was quick and lethal; here's the very next verse:

And there went out a fire from the Lord and devoured them and they died before the Lord.

It's hard to imagine such an atrocity played out in public. People have often enough told me this is an incomprehensible scene, that it's barbaric and shocking for them. They can imagine it: We live in the era when we all have seen the unspeakable, brain-exploding Zapruder film of the assassination of President John F. Kennedy, when we routinely view actual murders on television and the Web, and, more recently, the footage of horrifying acts of stoning, hangings, and beheadings.

It is likely many of these biblical-style incidents have been the ghoulish manifestations of "a fire from the Lord" thrust by human hands. Today, we call this "terrorism." The men and women committing these ferocities assert they are acting in God's name and that they enjoy heavenly sanction. So if you find it hard to believe God murdered those two boys for improvising the liturgy (as Jesus did every day), then you can certainly believe somebody in the crowd decided that Aaron's sons were out of line and savaged them. That's your "fire from the Lord."

Any way you look at this biblical episode, a foul bit of divinely driven homicide compressed into two sentences, it remains incongruous. It is the kind of thing that makes the strict sectarianism of then and now debilitating for the sophisticated, modern faith-seeker. I am skeptical about a spurious rabbinic justification for this tragedy: It happened to Aaron's overeager sons as a delayed punishment for Aaron's duplicity in the Golden Calf travesty.

Some theologians cite Paul's doctrine that there is "no respect of persons" and that anybody, regardless of station, is vulnerable to God's wrath if the divine law is flouted. There is also an assertion in Christianity that the fire sent by God to burn the priests was Christ coming to replace them. These kinds of raw and rough religious rationalizations are exactly the reason why so many bright and generous people are declaring they don't know what to believe.

I prefer to skip to the verses immediately following, which transfer the narrative from harsh mysticism right back into human hearts. The two youthful bodies still smoldering on the platform, Moses looks at Aaron and says:

This is what the Lord spoke, saying, I will be sanctified in them that come nigh unto me, and before all the people will be glorified.

In other words, "My brother, this is what happens to people who do my work but do it wrong because it represents me in the eyes of the crowd." From Moses to his brother, there are no words of solace, sympathy, or even consolation—just a pat response brimming with nauseating obeisance. And this, from the guy who vied and argued with God atop Mt. Sinai when God was about to destroy the whole of the people below for building the Golden Calf.

And here is exactly when and why the Bible works for me. Again, *this is life*: The same man who is noble and broadminded one day is an absolute iceberg on another day. The woman who is gracious on Monday is suddenly a study in boorishness on Wednesday. Your father was patient and accessible at one moment; he was inexplicably brusque and remote when you needed him next. Religion doesn't really thrive on fiery eruptions; religion was meant for human souls. And human souls are fluid, churning, exposed, and they are best understood as wells of uncertainty. If we are programmed to respond only to cataclysms, how on earth can we deal with the daily vicissitudes of real life? To burglaries, cancer treatments, miscarriages, cyber hackings, poor job evaluations, the deaths of longtime friends, and our own mounting apprehensions about mortality?

So Moses failed his brother at a moment of searing grief because his religious doctrine botched his thinking and choked his compassion. His spirit and his empathy ran aloof, and all he could do was fall back, feebly, on a theological pronouncement: "This is how the service is done and your sons did it another way, so that's that."

Aaron did better. Aaron—the one suffering the most—said nothing: "And Aaron held his peace," the Bible tells us. Yes, that's what happens when the people in our lives with whom we are closest, the ones who are supposed to understand and care about us unconditionally, inexplicably break our hearts. We become speechless. There are no words and there certainly are no platitudes. And when the Bible tells us about this difficult reality in the predicament of living, when it doesn't stand on ceremony, then the Bible becomes something you can believe.

⌒ℓ⌒

WHO WAS THE GREATEST spiritual pragmatist of all in scripture? Ironically, it may very well have been none other than God.

There's a remarkable bit of narrative at one point in the Book of Exodus, just after the Hebrew slaves escape from Egypt. They are on the move; they have literally walked through the parted Red Sea and, with pounding hearts and disbelieving eyes, witnessed the pursuing Egyptian chariot-men drowning in that sea. They've got hot sand blowing in their faces, and they are still unsettled, disconcerted, and afraid. Yet, it seems like this Moses and his God are gaining traction; they are gathering some kind of real initiative. The liberated slaves begin to bend ever so slightly into the desert wind. Moses and Aaron spread the word that the Promised Land is really only about two weeks away on foot. Their trajectory would take them on a fairly quick eastern trek along the Mediterranean coast. Sunlight and seagulls and the brisk salty air help lift their spirits a bit.

Then the Bible introduces a curious revelation:

Then it came to pass, when Pharaoh had let the people go, that God did not lead them by way of the land of the Philistines, although that was near; for God said, "Lest perhaps the people change their minds when they see war, and return to Egypt."

A Christian theologian, Richard Ritenbaugh, summarizes God's practical intuition about the immediate geographic/emotional challenge faced by Moses and his hosts as they escaped Pharaoh's grip: "The fledgling nation of Israel, God knew, was not yet prepared to fight any people as aggressive as the Philistines, no matter what their numbers were at the time."

So yes, even the Almighty can be a spiritual pragmatist in scripture. A god who makes realistic calculations, who takes into account the undeveloped skills and the raw trepidations of a people who were summarily converted from slaves into citizens—well, that's a god I can believe in. This is the kind of deity that feels for, rather than intimidates human beings. This is my God; this is the God who knows before we grew into practiced, accountable adults, we were innocent children who needed time and experience and a lot of patience before we could be thrust into precarious short cuts.

Remember the discussion of the spontaneous burst of prayer that came out of Rebekah, the deeply travailed mother-to-be of the twins, Jacob and Esau? In her physical anguish, Rebekah cried out to God, hoping to contravene her feelings of hopelessness. We later discover the mother, Rebekah, turns into the consummate spiritual pragmatist.

The twin boys were in their teenage years and suffered each other's presence. They were (like so many parents of two children have told me) as different as night and day. The Bible summarizes their dissimilarities in this way:

And the boys grew and Esau was a cunning hunter, a man of the field. And Jacob was a plain man, dwelling in tents.

So Esau was athletic, ruddy, and he loved the outdoors along with the smell and taste of wild game. In contrast, the rabbinic literature portrays Jacob as an inward, intellectual man who undoubtedly would have faithfully attended a desert Hebrew academy if there had been one. Jacob didn't earn any scouting merit badges in archery, backpacking, or woodcarving. He clung to his mother while Esau pleased his father Isaac's palate and machismo by cooking venison and "red pottage" and dancing by the fire.

In fact, Isaac favored Esau and was planning on passing along his birthright to the boy. This was appropriate; although the boys were twins, Esau had emerged first. This was what Isaac intended as he put us with his weak-chinned runner-up of a son, the momma's boy, Jacob.

Rebekah had other ideas, however. Isaac was getting on in years and the Bible tells us that he was losing his eyesight. So in another one of the more notorious stories in Genesis, the mother Rebekah conspires with her preferred Jacob to deceive Isaac and trick the old man into bequeathing the patrimony to him.

Rebekah cooked up some of her husband's favorite "savory meat" (the kind Esau normally brought to his father) and sent Jacob into Isaac's tent. But that was not all she did: She wrapped the pale Jacob's arms with goat hairs in order to impersonate the more robust Esau. And then Jacob proceeded to trick his father into thinking it was Esau in the tent and the unknowing Isaac inadvertently granted the birthright to Jacob.

Many commentators have conceded that Rebekah's actions were duplicitous and mendacious. It is hard not to call this little scheme dishonest, even cruel. But both the Jewish and Christian traditions were heartily serviced by this deception in the tent. The destiny of Israel and the pedigree of Christ were salvaged by it. It was the spiritual promises of both faiths to have Jacob (subsequently renamed "Israel" by God) inherit the theological future. A brave, if conniving mother knew which of her sons was better equipped to father Western religion.

So the lineage of our shared theologies was not created by any miraculous wonders wrought by heaven. No, it all happened because of a woman who was God's partner in spiritual pragmatism.

So why shouldn't you and I have faith in ourselves to believe so much in someone or something that we intervene when we know what is right? No one told Rebekah; she just got it. And she figured it out all by herself, against all custom, under the desert sky.

Chapter Eight

EVEN ABRAHAM LEARNED TO INCLUDE EVERYBODY

"There are as many ways to God as the breaths of the creatures."
—Ibn 'Arabi's Islamic Circle of Inclusion

IT'S NOT ABOUT HOW we treat God. It's about how we treat each other. That is the difference between religion and spirituality. God is not susceptible to our reach or our aggression. Other human beings certainly are—our children, neighbors, fellow motorists upon whom we dump road rage, and the endless list of international enemies we earn or accrue. It's become a cliché already that the biggest hypocrisy of organized religion is the divvying up of human status in the name of religion.

Remember the Islamic parable: Mohammed was in Medina with some of his comrades when a funeral procession passed by. The Prophet rose in respect. One of the companions pointed out that the deceased was a Jew. The Prophet replied, "Was he not a human being?"

Mohammed was not speaking from his liturgy at that moment. He was speaking from his heart. Would that every religionist, evangelist, and ideologue set aside the table of theological ordinances that skew this world every day and ask, "Is he or she not a human being?"

As a child living in Israel, I came to wonder (as did my schoolhouse friends) how it was that people in Europe had stopped considering certain other people as being human. This is because almost all of our elders— the teachers, the doctors, the street sweepers, and the shoemakers—were survivors of the Nazi Holocaust. They looked at us children through eyes seared with pain yet filled with a certain light. The light we noticed—even when we did not understand it—was the reflection of ourselves in their normally mournful eyes.

In those days, in that land, just several years after World War II, the fledgling Jewish State was a living national healing sanctuary. There was hardly an organized liturgy; this was a desert synagogue without walls. And we saw and experienced things that made us understand how much people can either help each other or hurt one another. We saw these people weep when a lemon tree was planted ceremoniously in front of a new public library or when we all would sing the national anthem, HaTikvah ("The Hope") before a local soccer game.

We youngsters lived naturally and comfortably with survivors of the genocide of six million Jews. They were real, fleshy, frequently tattooed (by their Nazi guards), and sometimes emotional. These former inmates of Treblinka, Bergen-Belsen, and Auschwitz were often new parents in a fresh land, who, by still being alive, defied what the Nazis had intended. They had survived because they were teenagers in the concentration camps—the demographic the Nazis more often spared because they could work. Taciturn, damaged, they looked after one another now with knowing glances and bitter nods, at least grateful for the freedom to think and reflect and even teach. What they taught was dignity and their classroom was the open air of a mystically safe place.

We children gained a sense of sanctity and survival from the numerous witnesses and sufferers who lived among us. They were moms and dads, bus drivers, ice cream vendors, mailmen, and booksellers.

Indeed, Old Man Binstock, who owned the town bookstore in the village square, had survived Dachau. His gray shop, where we purchased our school texts and note pads, always had that dusty-sweet smell of old tomes and wisdom. Each time Binstock handed over a Hebrew book of geography or literature to one of us kids, he'd say under his breath: "Another scoop of dirt in Hitler's grave."

And then there was Mr. Steiner. He was more mysterious than the others; we never really knew where he lived or what he did for a career. But in the fall of 1961, as we youngsters resumed our studies, we noticed the tall, wiry, and white-haired gentleman who met us every morning outside the schoolyard gate. He was kind and sweet, wounded somehow, yet grinning. We quickly learned that he enjoyed eating sunflower seeds.

It became a matter of pride for whichever one of us little boys provided Mr. Steiner with his daily bag of sunflower seeds. He was thankful for us in the morning and, as the wind blew in the scents of the nearby orange groves and onion fields, he would gently and ceremoniously tap each one of us on the top of our heads and pronounce a mantra of his own. It is engraved in our memories, wherever we are today.

One can only imagine the legal and social implications of this daily visit and contact with a "stranger" anywhere in America over fifty years later. But in Israel in 1961, we were not afraid of a smiling older man who liked to chat with us young boys about autumn rain, soccer, and sunflower seeds.

Although he never directly mentioned the Holocaust (nobody ever did), we understood he had something to do with it from two things: The SS-tattooed numbers on his forearm and the phrase he regularly used when he, in fact, tapped our heads good-bye for the morning.

Mr. Steiner would declare, looking into our faces and placing his wrinkled hands on us:

"You're not number six million and one."

Mr. Steiner smiled through his yellow teeth and one of us would reach up and carefully flick away some of the seed coverings that had fallen from his mouth and gotten caught in his whitish frizzled beard. He would laugh in a hollow kind of way—there was no voice left inside his soul. The citrus-scented breeze that faithfully drifted in from the groves the early settlers had planted decades before the European genocide brought with it the smell of rebirth. And we boys and Mr. Steiner understood each other as the wind came across from the Samarian Mountains.

None of us who were there in that situation have ever known such a prayer since.

THE SEARCH FOR GOD in that unpretentious time and place did not lead us to synagogues or to rabbis. It invariably directed us to shattered souls whom God had abandoned. Breathing the same air as such people, we found ourselves in heaven's schoolhouse. There was another gentleman in the village, much like Mr. Steiner, but unlike him in important ways. My buddies and I dubbed him "the sweet old man with the funny sun hat."

He was always there, in the clay house just beyond the trees. These were the trees of the forested field across the way from my grandmother's house—we looked out upon them across Jerusalem Street. Shrubs and wildflowers danced among the Lebanese cedars, oaks, and acacias. He was always there, the "elderly" man (he was but forty!), sweet as the oranges in his own tiny patch, with his yearning eyes and lonesome smile.

The thicket of saplings and shrubbery across the street was a favorite haunt of my friends, Roni, Yossi, and me. On carefree days, the Sabbath, or during the hot, muggy summer vacation, we'd often visit "the forest" and play in-between long shafts of sunlight. We had no iPads, no cellular phones, no Game Boys. Those gadgets were as far away as the celestials. We had each other, and the foliage of the Holy Land, and the feeling of being carefree and natural under the clouds. The trees gave shade and made us feel safe and special.

One of our favorite pastimes was to visit the forest after a matinee at the little cinema not far away on Jabotinsky Street. Almost always, we saw Tarzan movies—the exploits of the exotic and muscular "King of the Jungle" who flew through the jungles on vines, defeated alligators in the rivers, and always outsmarted the foreign and greedy hunters who came to Africa to kill wildlife and oppress the natives. The Tarzan movies, starring Johnny Weissmuller, were subtitled in Hebrew but the dialogue hardly mattered anyway. We just lived for Tarzan's trademark yell, as he swung through the African tropics and brought justice to wildlife and innocent people. Yossi was a specialist in mimicking the Tarzan howl. He would climb a mighty oak and belt out the call, with his Russian accent. We were happy and free, and we always knew of the nice neighbor who lived at the other end of the forest.

The sweet old man lived in a simple frame house that stood in a clearing and in-between clumps of forest. A dirt road wound its way from his home back to the main boulevard of our village. He had no wife and lived alone. The grown-ups spoke quietly about him, saying something about "the camps" and a daughter, and other things we did not understand then. When we saw him from a perch in the forest, we could sometimes see a strange tattoo of numbers on his forearm. I asked my grandmother about that, but strangely, she simply replied: "It's not time to tell you yet. But just be sure you are nice to him."

I understand now, of course, that the old man who lived by himself in the forest house had survived something called the Holocaust. No one else in his family survived, and he had come to Israel. Yossi's parents were like that; they had escaped separately from Europe after the nightmare but met in Israel. They both had lost all of their families and married in Kfar-Saba. Sometimes, Yossi would say, "I'm the new Israel." But he wasn't boasting. He was really proud, and so was I.

The sweet old man always wore a beaten, wrinkled sun hat. It seemed to be part of his body and it hung over the front of his brown and weathered face. His eyes were like two little stars glowing under the funny sun hat. The sweet old man had a few orange trees in the thicket, along the edge of the small field near his house. He did have a radio in the house, and we would occasionally hear classical music playing, with a lot of static, and sometimes news programs in a strange language.

Yossi and I would, from time to time, climb into the orange trees that belonged to the sweet old man. Like two friendly spies, we would seize one or two of the fruits and enjoy their juices. Sometimes, if we could secure good footing, we would peel and eat the fruit perched in one of the trees, acting like Tarzan's Jewish watchmen. We would wait for the sweet old man to acknowledge our petty larceny. This he did with his bell.

The bell, attached to the clay dwelling, could not be seen from the orange trees. It was located somewhere inside the house. The sweet old man would ring the bell every time—just to let us know he was aware we were enjoying his oranges. Whenever the bell rang into the little forest, Yossi and I would clap sticky hands, and we would feel that everything in the world was just fine.

Sometimes, before we would return home, we saw the sweet old man walking across his small field; the funny sun hat perched upon his head. He did not wave; the bell had already said hello. Yossi, Roni, and I never saw the sweet old man anywhere else in the village except around his field and his plain house.

One afternoon, Yossi and I were sitting in the trees, sharing an orange, watching the old man's house. We had been there for a while but, strangely, had not heard the bell ring this time. It was quiet, except for the muffled groaning of the Egged busses that came up and down the road just beyond the forest. The air was thick with citrus smells, though laced with a bit of the exhaust fumes that found their way over from Weizmann Boulevard. Yossi and I looked at each other, feeling a certain emptiness, even dread. "Do you think he died?" Yossi whispered to me. We were very concerned suddenly, and a little frightened. We decided to creep up close to the sweet old man's house.

Now we approached, squinting into the old man's windows. We peered into the main room. "Look!" cried Yossi, in an excited gasp. There, sitting on an ancient table, was the funny sun hat. It was like a cat, asleep and peaceful. Where was the old man? We tiptoed around to the next window.

"There you are, you two little outlaws!" The old man was laughing as he saw us from the inside. He stood in his narrow kitchen, stirring something. "Come in, come in," he urged, laughing again. "I have something for you."

The sweet old man was stirring tea boiling in a small pot. The tea bags, like our little world, were scented with orange. On a large, round plate there sat a stack of peanut cookies. "Look what I have for you two orange thieves who think I can't see you! Orange tea and cookies. Drink, and be welcome in my house."

The tea was warm and we blew it cool. Yossi and I giggled with delight. The sweet old man fed us the cookies; they were crunchy and delicious. He was so gentle and even knew our names. "Benny Kamin, I know your grandmother. Yona is a nice woman who waves to me from her porch when I walk by. I see you up there with her often, talking, reading, while she weaves those beautiful sweaters. Yossi Kluner, I know your father who drives that big oil tanker. Sometimes, when he gets home at night, you love to hop in and ride around the block with him before he finds a place to park that big thing."

"Yossi's father has let me ride in the truck, too!" I chimed in.

"I know, I know." The sweet old man had a very special twinkle in his eyes, as he used his right hand to rub the area of his left arm that carried that awful tattoo.

"We're sorry to have eaten some of your oranges," said Yossi.

"It's okay! Just leave me some for the market! And come back every day."

I asked him: "Why didn't you ring the bell today?"

"It was time to see how much you cared."

CARING ABOUT SOMEONE AND being interested in someone's well-being is a burst of spiritual clarity. These ethics do not stand at the door asking for a person's creed or the level of his intellect or whether or not she went to Harvard. The world we live in, with its cascading terrorism, its rampant sexual trafficking, its dying oceans and diseased forests, and—more benignly—its economic balkanization and social biases, requires something more than a bunch of recited sacraments. Human beings can no longer be complacent about the moral situation. And we cannot wait for God to save the day.

"Righteousness was asleep until it was awakened by Abraham," wrote the rabbis. Even the sages of old understood that God doesn't deliver beneficent outcomes; people inspired by God do. And they intuited enough to choose Abraham as the paradigm of this reality because only Abraham is revered paternally by all three of the Western faiths—Judaism, Christianity, and Islam.

I'm not saying we are all the same; blandness is not the element of an inclusive, creative spirituality that we can share. What I assert is that what we need is the same: A workable, believable personal theology is like a divine salad. The diversity of its ingredients, mixed together in a bowl of good intentions, makes for a unifying and nutritional spiritual outcome.

On June 10, 1963, just five months before he was assassinated, John F. Kennedy gave one of the most stirring speeches of his tragically short presidency. He spoke at the commencement ceremonies of American University in Washington and proposed that the United States and the then Soviet Union finally sign a treaty banning the further proliferation of nuclear weapons. Kennedy was known to have been deeply affected by the harrowingly close call of the Cuban Missile Crisis in 1962; historians generally agree the world came frighteningly close to an all-out atomic war between the two superpowers. That would have effectively ended human life on Earth.

Kennedy was many things—among them he was the young father of two small children. His biographers have made it clear that he had a tender place in his heart for youngsters; he could not bear the feeling of responsibility for a conflagration that would vaporize millions and millions of kids. At the university, the president made a stunningly spiritual plea that remains as eloquent as any Psalm: "For in the final analysis, our most basic common link is that we all inhabit this small planet. We all breathe the same air. We all cherish our children's futures. And we are all mortal."

John F. Kennedy was a Roman Catholic—the first to be elected president. He was not particularly religious and attended church intermittently and usually for political purposes. At American University on that June day, at the edge of his own mortality, he spoke from the deepest part of his soul and surely spoke for the God we should all worship.

Meanwhile, regardless of its affiliation, a House of God is just that. Years ago, after a synagogue in Cleveland abruptly dismissed me as its spiritual leader, I discovered tenderness and healing in a regal old church.

My older daughter and I were returning from what had been a pleasant, but painfully revealing meeting, with the top editors of the *Cleveland Plain Dealer*. It was about two weeks after the discharge. My daughter was twenty years old at the time, home on winter college break, doing her best to soothe her father's pain and humiliation over the dismissal. The paper's publisher had invited me to a meeting with a few top editors with the intent of discussing a position as a fulltime columnist. It was a very curative and soothing gathering; I took to heart the unmitigated kindness of this group of all-Christian executives. There was notable shock and outrage in the community about my firing and this meeting salved my feelings.

Driving up Cleveland's stately and hilly eastern suburban streets, a kind stillness in the car between us, I noticed my daughter staring out into the snowy world—a look of incomprehension and fear shaping her face. The executives at the *Plain Dealer* had been so thoughtful and compassionate: I was a regular contributor of columns and they really wanted to do something to help.

But in spite of the coffee and cakes and genuinely nice talk, there was really no future for me right then as a suddenly remade journalist.

My heart ached for my daughter, in fact for both of my daughters, who were suffering through this rather public event at the time. And I wasn't without my own deep mortification and apprehensions and anger; I yearned for a spiritual mentor to comfort my daughter and me. Someone to listen and not offer impossible clichés; someone who could offer insight from the wisdom of the real world and not stand on gratuitous aphorisms; someone whose soul was in scripture but who understood about families and fathers and job loss and marriage and degradation. Someone who wasn't parochial about denomination.

I found myself pulling into the driveway of St. Paul's Episcopal Church in Cleveland Heights. I had no idea if the rector, Reverend Nick White, a dear friend and longtime community partner, was even available or if this was acceptable protocol. But I was really in trouble.

We walked into that Christian sanctuary, where I had often preached and taught, and spoke to an immediately welcoming receptionist, who was not certain if Reverend White was in the building. I apologized for the presumption; it just felt like a balm to be so warmly received. The receptionist made a couple of hushed calls on her intercom; in moments, we were being accompanied up an obscured staircase to what was Nick White's unassuming private study. (I later learned he had left a meeting in session to meet us the second he heard we were in the church).

He joined us and spoke quietly to us while warming the room with a kettle of steaming tea and asked gently probing questions to my daughter. He hoped these questions would soften the stones in my soul. "How do you think your dad is doing?" "Are you angry at anybody?" "Would you like to call me when you get back to school so we can speak privately?"

There was no discussion that afternoon about God, faith, and theology, and there was certainly no judgment. I was not pressed for any Episcopalian credentials. The holy man merely wanted to be kind. I added this awareness to what I call spiritual pragmatism—the preacher was there for me just because the circumstances threw us together and I needed help.

For those who think the regimens of old religion imply strict compliances and narrow categories of acceptance, I refer to a story found in Talmudic literature—some 2,000 years in existence. Again, our hero is Abraham, and the "liberal voice" admonishing him is that of none other than God.

Abraham and Sarah were the parents of monotheism, the belief that there is one, unseen God. They pioneered the Star of David, the Cross, and the Star and Crescent. This assessment of them is at the core of all three "Abrahamic" faiths. In the Old Testament, the deity instructs this nomadic couple, who have abundant cattle and great wealth, to remove themselves from their native home. "Go to a land that I will show you." They would travel from Mesopotamia (now Iraq) to that land, Canaan, which eventually became Israel. Nobody knows why God picked Abraham and Sarah but neither can anybody explain why the faith system they created has become, at once, the most poetic and bloody business ever devised in human history.

This little yarn from the rabbinic books of wisdom, while establishing an exalted principle, may also give us a clue as to why religious zeal is so dangerous. It is also an example of a religious doctrine one can embrace and believe.

Abraham was settling down to sleep in a corner of his oversized tent. He and Sarah and their vast array of sub-lords and servants were well on their way to "a new land." Sarah slumbered against the opposite side of the enclosure, among several handmaidens who attended to her and had lulled her to sleep with fine oils massaged on her forehead and unto her feet. Abraham looked out through the flap; the stars displayed like crystal blazes in the clear-black desert sky. The wind was low. *Good*, thought the patriarch.

He was far away from home along the banks of the Euphrates River in the land of Ur, in southern Mesopotamia. He was nonetheless possessed with a sense of mission; he had renounced the pagan idols of his upbringing and felt moved and directed by this unseen god that charged him to undertake this journey.

Abraham stirred the barley soup that boiled above a fire in the corner of the tent. He slurped a last steaming ladle-full of it and then enjoyed a piece of flatbread that he crisped over the fire. He drank some cactus wine from a flask made of sheepskin. He relished the warmth of the nectar as it sank into his body. He lay down in his roll of wool-woven blankets and contemplated sleep.

A few hours later, Abraham was awakened by a man's voice calling from just outside the tent. "May I enter, my lord?" The man spoke in a Bedouin tongue. Abraham stirred himself up and stepped outside onto the entrance—a long heavy flap conveyed by thick poles and ropes. It was deep into the night, but the moon lit up the entranceway and Abraham could see the face of a hungry desert wayfarer in need of some comfort and rest.

"I am pleased to invite you into my tent," said the patriarch, instinctively acting upon traditional wilderness hospitality. He helped the man with his pouches and sacks and led him inside. Abraham gave the visitor some bread and wine and designated a place for him to sleep in an adjacent corner of the tent. The man bowed incessantly and expressed his gratitude.

Abraham, satisfied that he had done the right thing, lulled himself back to sleep.

Just moments after he dozed off, he was awakened by a peculiar sound. The visitor was chanting some kind of unfamiliar devotion while looking upward and swaying his body in a ritualistic fashion that Abraham did not recognize. Abraham arose and felt a burst of anger and resentment. This man was a pagan!

Abraham marched toward his visitor and demanded of him: "What are you doing?"

The man trembled in fear but replied: "I am thanking my gods for your kindness, sir."

Abraham was not impressed. "His gods?" This was the tent of Yahweh—the one and supreme God that had specifically anointed Abraham and Sarah to lead the way to a new and true faith. No pagans allowed in this tent.

"Get out!" Abraham was seething. "Out!" The man was terrified and speedily collected his meager belongings and fled the tent. Abraham, still panting with rage, watched the man's figure in the fading moonlight until he disappeared across the sand dunes.

Abraham returned to his blankets feeling smug and satisfied. "That's exactly what God would want me to do," he thought to himself.

He was about to doze off when now he heard another kind of voice altogether.

"Abraham!"

Abraham was hearing God's voice.

"Yes, Lord?" Abraham was sure that God was going to praise him for cleansing the tent of a nonbeliever.

"What did you just do?"

"I sent the man out because he is a pagan. He doesn't believe in you the way we do and doesn't deserve to stay in our tent."

"I see. Tell me, Abraham, about how old do you think your visitor was?"

"How old? I'd say, about twenty-five years old."

"Un-huh. So I've put up with that man's religion for twenty-five years and you couldn't bear him for one night?"

Abraham now quivered. He was speechless. God spoke one more time:

"Get up out of your bed and run out into the desert and find that man. Bring him back and apologize and then make sure he's warm and well fed. If there isn't room for anybody in your tent, then you have not heard me in the first place."

THE MAN WHO INVENTED GOD

*"And who could find such a man,
in whom there is the spirit of God?"*
—PHARAOH OF EGYPT AS QUOTED
IN THE BOOK OF EXODUS

IN MANY WAYS, GOD is the longest-running rumor in human history. You did not become aware of God because you got a nudge in the back from some heavenly source or had light thrown into your eyes by a celestial being. You are aware of God because somebody told you about God. A parent, a minister, a teacher—someone in a position of authority or influence conveyed this notion of a heavenly creator to you in the course of your experience.

Neither you nor I have ever received an email, an express package, or any kind of oracle directly from on high. If you are convinced that God exists in one way or another, you are persuaded because of the inspiration or philosophy of some other person or persons.

Even the hard fundamentalists didn't discover their punishing version of God because they opened a holy book and read about it. They have all been pushed into submission on this issue and this interpretation because other zealots pounded it into them and made it legitimate and safe.

Few of us can pinpoint the moment when we first heard about the divine order of things. I recall my mother explaining to me one day, when I was eight or nine years old, that when each one of us is born, God places a little piece of himself within us and that is our soul. This little bit of childhood theology was comforting and gentle, and it has served me well enough that I occasionally share it with other people. There are simply no absolute truths in this matter but there are undeniably many moments when each one of us needs something that feels true.

Living each day, rushing to work, getting through the pressures and responsibilities of being a partner or a parent or just doing it alone—we don't really reflect that much about the existence of God. Balancing the checkbook is more on our minds than pleasing the Almighty. This is because life is normally programmed and generally uneventful. We bow to bosses, calendars, and infirmities. We spend a lot more time with the grocery list than a prayer list. Most people who come along and start rambling to us about God in the middle of the day we dismiss as, well, crazy. Really? You're preaching to me about heaven while I'm just trying to figure out how this world works? Our skepticism and lack of interest is understandable; we're trying to make ends meet and doing our best with the cards handed to us by reality.

We are busy; we compete for space on the highway, at the office, in shopping malls, and we submit to the controlled current of existence. The drone of life blocks most of the spiritual dimensions; we accede to logic, statistics, and to credit ratings. Our senses have been dulled: We rely upon manufactured machines and devices to supply us with information, entertainment, pleasure, and diversion.

Reverend Donald Sage Mackay, a Christian reformer who lived in New York City, wrote in 1902: "For tens of thousands of toilers in this city, the humdrum monotony of each day . . . is just a going out in the morning to labor and a coming in at evening to rest." This resonates even more so in the twenty-first century as we reboot, record "on-demand," copy and paste, print, buy, and then upgrade our cell phones. Before long, our automobiles, equipped with Wi-Fi hotspots, will be driving without any assistance from us.

So we're not looking for proof of God until life hurts us. Bam! God is the bursting yield of a crisis, prayer is the language of discomfort, and faith is the product of limitations. God has been programmed out of our consciousness until we need something more than we can download. "A higher being" is someone we ache for when we can no longer tolerate the routinizing of spirit that organized religion commands.

And yet, even when we are possibly confronted by some kind of divine manifestation, some improbable event to which we might ascribe God's hand—a close call on the freeway, an astonishing recovery from a dreaded illness—we are cautioned to restrain our religious zeal. Where is such a caution? The answer: in the Scripture itself. Even the Bible records the healthy cynicism of human beings allegedly witnessing miracles. Giving it all to God can lead to inflated expectations down the line.

The Hebrew slaves had been free for only a short time when they came scurrying to the shores of the Red Sea. They were panting and out of breath as the sea salt stung their eyes and their implausible new situation spun their heads. They may not have known that Egyptian warriors were in pursuit and planned to slaughter them at the shores in revenge for their slipping out of Pharaoh's dominion. Nonetheless, they had just observed a lot of wonders, so pathetically lost upon them.

The Hebrews had directly witnessed the Ten Plagues inflicted upon the Egyptians—a catalog of catastrophes ranging from hail to daytime darkness to locusts to frog infestation to a blood-drenched Nile to the final, horrific slaughter of all Egyptian first-born children. (The Jewish tradition is uncomfortable about that and requires participants at the Passover Seder to remove ten drops of wine from everyone's glass in remembrance of Egyptian suffering at that time.)

One would think seeing all those horrors wrought upon their longtime taskmasters would have convinced the exiting Hebrews that God was for real. Not necessarily. They weren't even ready to commit unconditionally to God after personally experiencing the parting of the Red Sea. Yes, they crossed over on the soggy floor of the sea just in time to escape the approaching Egyptian chariots. Yes, they watched from the other side as the trailing militiamen drowned in the returning waters. Yes, they sang a liberation song under the guidance of Miriam, Moses's sister, who danced and played her tambourine. But here is what they sang—it's right there in the Book of Exodus:

Who among the gods is like you, Lord? Who is like you—majestic
in holiness, awesome in glory, working wonders?

"Among the gods?" In their rhapsody, that's the best they could do? Ascribe to God a conditional status, implying they still affirmed the existence of other deities? Here is the climactic moment of the Hebrew freedom ride, the phenomenal culmination of sweeping events, the mass engulfing of their lethal pursuers, and their own escape and survival. And the best the Hebrews could do is chant: "Good job, God. You're a contender! You get great marks among the various divinities."

I'm not suggesting this faint praise by the Hebrews was a worthy assessment, given the immediate circumstances. But I am suggesting that people can witness remarkable things externally and still not be entirely convinced about God. And I am illustrating this irony with an incident that is not only published in the Bible, but remains one of the key moments in the entire chronicle.

Maybe the real proof of God comes from within rather than without. In other words, where does God actually exist, really live, truly work? There is a pattern of comparable responses in the major Western religions and it supersedes all the ceremonials. Where is God?

The answer from the Jewish tradition: wherever we let him in.

From Christianity: in your heart.

From Islam: whenever you feel oneness with the world around you.

So, the organized faiths basically agree that all the miracles, cataclysms, upheavals, and apocalypses notwithstanding, God lives inside us. God exists when people tell each other about him.

One of the great heroes of the Old Testament was neither a Christian nor a Jew nor a Muslim. His name was Jethro. Besides being the high priest of the desert Midianite people, Jethro was also the father-in-law of Moses. The man was a major pagan, yet he had exclusive family connections to the founding rabbi of the Jewish people and the portion of Torah that includes the Ten Commandments is actually named "Jethro!" (Here is another shining example of religious inclusiveness in an ancient tradition shared by Christians, Muslims, and Jews.)

In the biblical text, there is a small, poignant story of family tenderness that directly precedes the big theater of the Ten Commandments on the mountain. Following the escape via the Red Sea, Moses returns to Midian, where his wife and sons were living. I favor this little anecdote because it reveals the all-too-often neglected scriptural capacity for humane and compassionate interactions among those characters we regularly put on pedestals.

Moses is coming home after a hard adventure. It doesn't matter how eminent or esteemed a person is. When he or she returns to the familiar and reassuring environment of house and family, especially after surviving a heady and dangerous and historic experience, that person wants to talk about it. He wants to decompress in a safe place, away from the glare of the press and the fulmination of the critics. Moses was looking to share it all with a father or at least his father-in-law, given that Moses no longer had his parents. We need love more than we need law. We want the approval of our elders more than we require their religious biases.

In the text, the following is written:

And Moses went out to meet his father-in-law, and paid his respects, and kissed him. They asked each other about their welfare and they went into the tent.

No frills here, no spectacle, and no mystery. The younger man just wants to unwind with his paternal figure and discuss what he had been through. This has happened to you and me countless times—with a dad, a mom, a grandparent, or another elder. You came home from college. You returned from war. You completed an appearance in court. You ended it with a spouse. You discovered a job is not working out or you lost the position altogether. You want to bare your soul, and you have to do it in a safe place. Here's the next sentence in the scripture:

And Moses told his father-in-law all that God had done to Pharaoh and to the Egyptians for Israel's sake. And all the travail they had experienced and how God delivered them.

One can almost see Moses in the tent unwinding, unloading, remembering, and putting it all together for himself and his sympathetic listener with no buffer, no judgment, and no fear of reprisal. It was likely cathartic: the recollections of confronting Pharaoh in the palace court, his own vulnerability at such moments, his fear of incarceration or worse, the doubts he surely had about this God that sent him would protect him. The skepticism of the Hebrews—even the downright hostility of some of them, who feared and resented Moses's stirring up trouble for them— already in a precarious situation and totally helpless against the Egyptian police establishment. If you can't tell your father you were scared, then whom can you tell?

And Jethro listens. There is no quote attributed to him in the text until his son-in-law is finished unburdening himself. He heeds the wonderment and awe and trepidations pouring out of his son-in-law's soul. And he also hears something else that has a profound effect upon the older man. Moses's testimony is so vivid and heartfelt (and the trust between the two men so deep) that the elder has an epiphany, strictly based on what he's being told:

> Now I know that God is greater than all the gods, for he did this to those who had treated Israel arrogantly.

"God is greater than all the gods," declared the pagan high priest who had no prior knowledge of God or hadn't seen the miracles and wonders. He was being told the story by the young man he loved, the husband of his daughter. And he believed in God without the conditions put on God by the Hebrews who had literally passed through all those events—the ones who danced and sang along the Red Sea and declared that God was a deity among the Gods.

We don't need theological smoke and mirrors or even high liturgies to believe in God, if we have such a conviction at all. That's not how it happens, not in the real world of human life. We discover God because someone we trust told us about him, and we were convinced because the conversation was natural, unstructured, and shared, not decreed.

I don't think it was Moses who discovered God. Nor was it Jesus or Sarah or Noah or the great prophet Deborah. In all of these instances, according to the narrative we find in the scriptural texts, *God discovers* these people. They hear from angels, oracles, intermediaries, or they undergo supernatural events that persuade or convert them to such a revelation. So this is not discovering—it is encountering. Such encounters often result in good things; we certainly want Moses to be inspired, whether by a burning bush or any necessary medium, to leave Midian and return to Egypt in order to free the slaves. But Moses did not find God. God found him.

It's a whole different story with Joseph. The shamelessly favored son of Jacob, the one whose personal conceit and narcissism earned him the scorn of his eleven brothers, Joseph is nonetheless the man who discovered God. His story, which takes place primarily in Egypt, and occupies the final thirteen chapters of the Book of Genesis, is unique.

Joseph suffers a lot and overcomes almost every adversity. His brothers are driven into a jealous rage by the manner in which their father fawns over Joseph. When Jacob exclusively presents Joseph with a multicolored coat (a symbol of supremacy in the ancient Middle East), the lad unwisely flaunts it. He taunts his brothers, telling them that they are poor farmers and their dreams have no value. The Bible is working for me here: Sibling rivalry and family dysfunction are endemic to human life, much more so than thundering supernatural events and divine disasters. The brothers conspire to kill him. That family members would murder one another is more believable to me than God opening the earth and having it devour a bunch of alleged sinners.

Joseph survives the attempted fratricide; he endures in an open desert pit, outlasting hunger, heat, and pests. He is found, unearthed, then bound and held captive by desert bandits and subsequently sold into house servitude in Egypt. He refuses the sexual advances made by the restive wife of the Egyptian nobleman where he is confined. Humiliated, the spiteful woman claims impropriety and the young man is thrown into state prison without recourse. Through all these trials, Joseph is talking to himself about God. But not once does the Bible indicate that God ever says a single word to Joseph. No signs, no interventions, no signals, nothing at all comes to Joseph from above.

One might ask: Why is this guy in the Bible? He's not interacting with heaven, and he's not hearing anything from above. He's on his own exactly when he's having the worst troubles. Wait, isn't that just like it is for you and me?

It's in prison where Joseph discovers his own power to generate God. Unlike no one else in the entire scripture, he has nothing to go on but his own intuition and inner belief system. He is bequeathed no "signs and wonders." In fact, the environment of his God-awareness is replete with dark cells, misery, tawdry fellow inmates, brutish guards, and the unyielding stigma of being a despised Hebrew in the world of elitist Egyptians.

Acting on his own wits and savvy, Joseph takes up the art of interpreting other people's dreams while he's in jail. Two of Pharaoh's former employees, a baker and a butler, are in the same compound as Joseph. The two unfortunate men had offended the king. They are possessed by inexplicable dreams and are drawn to the charismatic Joseph. The Bible presents the following:

> And they said to him, "We each have had a dream, and there is no interpreter of it." So Joseph said to them, "Do not interpretations belong to God? Tell them to me, please."

"Do not interpretations belong to God?" Joseph is as vain about his intuition as he is sincere in feeling he is in touch with God's sensibilities. In other words: Talk to me; you're learning about God.

Joseph offers the butler a favorable interpretation of that man's dream: Pharaoh will forgive him and he will be restored to his palace position in three days (which is what comes to pass). But Joseph has a bit more on his agenda. In exchange for this information, he wants the freed butler to work for his own release.

> But remember me when it is well with you, and please show kindness to me. Make mention of me to Pharaoh, and get me out of this house. For indeed I was stolen away from the land of the Hebrews; and also I have done nothing here that they should put me into the dungeon.

It's a different story for the poor baker:

> When the baker saw that the interpretation was good, he said to Joseph, "I also was in my dream, and there were three white baskets on my head. In the uppermost basket were all kinds of baked goods for Pharaoh, and the birds ate them out of the basket on my head." So Joseph answered and said, "This is the interpretation of it: The three baskets are three days. Within three days Pharaoh will lift off your head from you and hang you on a tree; and the birds will eat your flesh from you.

So while the outcome would be starkly different for those two fellow inmates, Joseph nailed it all with his prophecies. The liberated butler forgot about Joseph immediately after rejoicing in his own restored status, but Joseph's reputation as a clairvoyant would nonetheless pay off for him. The next thing you know, Pharaoh himself is having strange dreams and is walking around the palace in a state of panic. The exact words in scripture are that "his spirit was troubled."

The king's sleep was disturbed by inexplicable visions of seven fat cows and then seven lean cows along the river, as well as a parallel apparition of healthy and pallid stalks of corn. What did it mean? Pharaoh ranted at his sages and magicians but nobody could offer an answer. It was not a pleasant interlude in the palace and people were quivering for their careers—and their lives.

Enter the butler, the former inmate, who suddenly remembered the poised Hebrew soothsayer who had interpreted dreams so accurately in the penitentiary. The butler was careful before he spoke up: "Forgive me all my faults, Pharaoh. But I know this man from prison who is amazing with dreams."

"Get him over here!" Pharaoh was feverish.

The Bible, which can fluently move from mountaintop marvels to very intimate incidentals, describes Joseph's inner excitement when he gets the summons:

> And they brought him hastily out of the dungeon. He shaved himself
> and changed his clothes and then appeared before Pharaoh.

Pharaoh told him about his dreams and growled: "There's just nobody here who can interpret them." The attending courtiers shook in their sandals and trembled in their kilts as Pharaoh bristled under his white crown and beneath his leopard skins. The king invited Joseph to talk—something the young Hebrew was always eager to do.

Joseph was not starstruck; he confidently declared to Pharaoh that he had the complete analysis of the dreams. Not to worry. However, it had to be understood that it was not really Joseph talking but God. God was communicating through Joseph. Okay, Pharaoh, so you saw seven fat cows and then seven lean cows? Got it. Then you envisioned seven full stalks of corn and then seven withered stalks of corn? No problem. God has conveyed a prophecy, and I'm just the guy delivering the message.

Joseph declared, "The dreams are one. God is showing Pharaoh what to do." Focusing on the numerology of the king's night terrors, Joseph then explicated:

> *The seven good cows are seven years and the seven good ears of corn are seven years. And the seven thin and ill-favored cows that came after them are seven years. The seven empty ears of corn blasted with the east wind shall be seven years of famine.*

Joseph went on with clarity in both his vision and his voice. Egypt was about to enjoy seven years of "great plenty" but then immediately suffer seven years of "grievous famine." The doubling of imagery (cows and corn) was a seal of God's authorship of the dreams. So the thing to do, Joseph self-assuredly directed Pharaoh, was to store up extra food during the years of plenty. That way, the famine's severity would be mitigated and the people would not be hungry. And they would not be prone to insurrection.

Only an hour earlier, this Hebrew fellow had been wallowing in jail. Now Pharaoh was listening to him with fascination and respect. Joseph was not quite finished with his discourse, however. Having interpreted the dream, he then pushed the envelope with a practical suggestion:

> *Now let Pharaoh look out for a man discreet and wise and set this man over the land of Egypt.*

Pharaoh didn't have to check out anybody on LinkedIn or even wait for a CV. Joseph, an imaginative amalgam of charisma and chutzpah, had everything under control. Here's the job description, and I'm the man for the job. What are you waiting for, Pharaoh?

In that moment, Joseph of the Bible was the quintessential spiritual pragmatist. He drew from his inner life with God and applied it to both the economic dangers facing his host nation, as well as his audacious employment application. Responding to all this moxie and morality, Pharaoh, quite struck by all of it, looked around the gallery and exclaimed to his palace officers:

And who could find such a man, in whom there is the spirit of God?

"The spirit of God?" Pharaoh had absolutely no prior knowledge or awareness of God! In Egypt, the sun was God. In some ways, Pharaoh himself was the deity. What was Pharaoh doing, suddenly invoking "the spirit of God?" This is either a scriptural error or, just maybe, an epiphany.

The bottom line here: Pharaoh learned about God because Joseph told him about God. Just like my mother revealed God to me when I was a child and somebody in your life unveiled God to you in a story, a parable, or a personal aphorism. For both you and me, that moment long predated the first time you recited about God in a devotional book or even some holy writ.

This is much like Moses when he was a young shepherd, just before he found himself compelled by the voice he "heard" at the Burning Bush to return to Egypt and become the world's first civil rights leader. The incident makes sense to me when one construes it as a question of a man hearing his inner voice driving him to do God's work—in this case, to go out and free some people. Martin Luther King, Jr. spoke of a profoundly dark midnight for himself during the difficult and dangerous days and nights of the 1955 bus boycott in Montgomery, Alabama.

King was deeply frightened and apprehensive for his young family and himself. Dreadful, anonymous phone calls persisted at home from ghoulish people threatening to murder him, his wife, and his children.

His house was bombed one night. He needed faith. He needed hope. He did not receive these from a cosmic omen that suddenly appeared at his kitchen table where he sat with his head in his hands, trying to hold back tears and panic.

King described this to his congregation in a preachment called "A Knock at Midnight." At the very instant when his soul was barren of any courage and ravaged by despair, King sensed, from deep inside himself, the inspiration of something divine. Like Joseph, he found God from within. And then he went out and told America about what God wanted.

In our own journeys, each one of us discovers God (specifically, our individual concepts of God) in our private "Burning Bush moments." These breakthrough moments happen when somebody is enlightening you or when you realize an interior supplication—not when something is on fire or a sea is parting or a genocidal deity is opening the earth to swallow up a population of sinners. A father's words, a grandmother's steaming soup, a child's recognition of your love, a teacher's intuition, a spouse's hand on your back—these are the settings in which God lives.

⁘

"GOD WAS IN THE boxcars."

A few years ago, I was introduced to a most unusual man. Lou Dunst, now approaching the age of ninety, is a religiously observant man who saved his own soul. Between the ages of fourteen and nineteen, Lou survived four Nazi death camps and two failed gas chamber incidents. For decades, he has been a grateful creature of the synagogue but he found God—and his ability to survive—in a place that had nothing to do with God.

It's one thing to visit in a synagogue and talk with God about life and death, fate and fortune, mortality and miracles, cruelty and compassion. It's another thing to share this conversation with a kindly man who has experienced all of these things and could easily debate with God on every score.

It was on the Jewish Sabbath when I was invited to first sit with Lou, consecrate life at his side, chant the blessing over the Torah scroll as he watched, and mourn the dead in the same cadenced devotion as this man who survived the Kingdom of Death and today is an inspirational speaker for tolerance and forgiveness. Lou wanted me to write his life story.

Lou has traveled the world with his account of both unimaginable horrors and mind-boggling survival; he has inspired youngsters to do good works and he has moved police officers and Navy Seals to tears and reflection. He needs to tell the story, I think, or the story will consume him.

What do you think about when you commiserate about God next to a man who doesn't understand why God spared him as the world was choking and smoldering with hatred and murder? That there really is a God? That God is an illusion, a device for the rationalization of the most ungodly things? That life is the most hopeless of enterprises where evil wins and hate vanquishes and violence reigns and war is unchecked?

Or that life is the most precious of things, made sacred by each breath of a kindly man who was dug out, all but lifeless, from among a tower of corpses stinking of death and thrown into the sewers of the netherworld? This, while the Allies advanced with their tanks and the Germans retreated with their secrets.

"I'm not an educated man," said Lou to me in almost a whisper. "You know, the Germans closed the schools to us." Indeed. Jewish children were banned from schools, playgrounds, ice cream shops, and from having books, shoes, hopes, and dreams. The Gestapo would roam the streets of Poland, Romania, Czechoslovakia, and many other nations, randomly shooting kids, raping their sisters, and beating their fathers to death. Their crime: being Jewish.

Lou survived, in an astounding escape from the pyramid of the dead, by virtue of a valorous and quick-thinking US serviceman, as well as the uncanny search through the right pile of corpses just in the nick of time by his own brother. He has dedicated his life for the last seventy years to charity, education, restoring burnt Torah scrolls, and rebuilding devastated synagogues in Europe and elsewhere. I asked Lou why he does it. He remembered finding God over and over again within himself, in the camps, during the shootings and mass beatings, while burning with starvation, clamoring for his murdered parents, and fighting off thoughts of suicide. At one point, he discovered a mantra coming from the most primal part of his being: "I was delirious and just cried out to God, 'Let me live so I can tell the story!'"

There was no synagogue from within to make this plea. No retreat center or meditation pagoda. Just shooting fields, hideaway holes and caves, mass graves, torture chambers, reeking ghettos, and—in-between such places and the death camps—the unspeakable, moving, enclosed, choking, rancid railroad cars in which the Jews were packed that were called boxcars.

Lou recounted that early in the nightmare, he and his family were locked within the Mátészalka (Hungary) Ghetto. Then suddenly, they were again thrust into boxcars.

He told me, "This time it was even worse. We were sick and weak and diseased. We had diarrhea and dehydration and the conditions in the rail car—when I talk about it, I can't even believe the things I am actually remembering. Day after day, off we went. We were pressed together like animals. Sometimes the train would stop for hours and hours, and we were gasping for air in the heat, with no light, no water, nothing. They had to stop because the rails did not match the wheels. Or they were hooking up other cars from who knows where. From other cities, even other countries. In the car, some people were dying and some were dead. Some were giving birth but it had to be done in a way that nobody from the Nazis should see because, as in the ghetto, pregnant woman were shot. If you didn't run fast enough when they wanted you to go from here to there, boom! Shot. No questions. No thinking. To them, Jewish life was cheap. Everything they felt like doing, they did it. And always, they were yelling 'Schnell!' We had to move fast. I saw people— men, women, and children—shot dead in front of me because they didn't move fast enough or they just looked the wrong way. We were again in the boxcars. But somehow I believed, even in there, God was in those boxcars."

I swallowed in disbelief as the cherubic, friendly man related this to me, his eyes still somehow sweet with hope. He was wearing his prayer shawl and skullcap and tenderly holding onto his prayer book. He had been Joseph in the pit, though this pit was as wide as Europe and as deep as the deepest racism ever manifested in the long, wretched history of human hate. "Lou," I asked, "How did you pray in such a situation? You had no prayer book and, even if you did, there was no safe place to go and pray."

"My soul was my prayer book. It was always safe to go there."

Chapter Ten

GOD GETS IT THAT
WE'RE FLAWED

*"Alas! Those good old days are gone, when a murderer could wipe the stain
from his name and soothe his trouble to sleep simply by getting out
his blocks and mortar and building an addition to a church."*
—MARK TWAIN

GERTRUDE AND PHILIP MENDELSOHN were friends of my parents during the 1960s in Cincinnati. They were tolerant, suburban, middle-class, progressive Jewish-types who supported a folksy synagogue in an outlying section of town aptly called "Northern Hills." They loosely kept kosher, basically not mixing meat and milk products at home though enjoying unrestricted Chinese food "outside the house"—a classic modern hypocrisy that is nonetheless a hallmark of spiritual pragmatism.

Just because the Mendelsohns ate pork ribs and shrimp rolls on Sunday nights did not mean they weren't supporting myriad charitable social causes all week long, from hunger projects to an interfaith homeless center to a battered women's shelter.

The Mendelsohns solemnly lit the Sabbath candles with their three children on Friday evening if Philip got home on time from his job as a high school guidance counselor near downtown. They pulled out their coffee-stained, "Maxwell House" Haggadah books for their annual at-home Passover Seder meal and ritual with family and friends. They sang, ate, and debated heartily around the table about freedom, slavery, plagues, miracles, and gods.

Like most American Jews, they barely understood any of the Hebrew spoken and chanted during the services at their synagogue but enjoyed "the feeling" in the sanctuary and the general sense of ancestral fellowship. This does not really differ from what many of my Catholic friends relate: They don't necessarily comprehend the Latin-intoned mystique of their traditional liturgy but they feel a cultural comfort zone in the neighborhood church setting.

The Mendelsohn family lived on a manicured lawn property with a concrete driveway leading up to an imposing if faceless, gray, two-car garage for their two Chevrolets. Their tract-style home contained squeak-proof flooring, lath and plaster walls ("Not drywall!" bellowed Philip), furniture from Sears, and several noisy, Trane air conditioning units that hung precariously outside their windows. These delivered intermittent relief from the unrelentingly humid Cincinnati summers. Philip steadfastly hung a US flag outside the front stoop every legal holiday but also kept an oversize flag of Israel tacked by its corners across one of the garage walls.

I loved those people and thought they had a good deal going with God.

Gertrude, with short dark hair and deep hazel eyes, was wiry and vaguely attractive; Philip was thick and heavy-shouldered with teddy-bear cheeks and big hands he used to heartily embrace people or to punctuate his robust political statements. He had no patience for social façades and he railed against those who "helped commit the crimes with their silence." He wept openly when my family visited the Mendelsohns on the morning of June 6, 1968 when Senator Robert F. Kennedy died from his gunshot wounds.

"A year ago we were dancing in the street after Israel whipped the Arabs in the Six Day War," heaved Philip. "My God, this country of ours is going to hell. We just buried Martin Luther King two months ago." Gertrude used her small hands to wipe his large face, which was dripping with tears and perspiration.

Philip looked at me and said, "You see, Ben, people are nuts. People are flawed. In fact that's why I like the Bible so much."

"What?" I asked. Philip had calmed down and now he was ready to begin a spiritual discourse. Philip Mendelsohn, whom I thoroughly adored for his enthusiasm and fealty to young people, and who fancied himself as a kind of suburban Jewish deacon, proceeded to edify me with something that has clarified my relationship with the scripture ever since.

"What do you mean, 'What'?" Now Philip was gaining his steam, his eyes brightened and his hands waved in the air. "I can live with this world because everybody, every hero in the Bible is flawed. Haven't you ever noticed this? Killers, philanderers, nut cases. Neurotic kings. People fighting off depression. That's why I can relate to it. The people in the Bible are authentic, so they make this world make sense. We are just like them."

Philip stepped back to regard me and to discern whether I understood what he had just said. In fact, it went through me like a diamond bullet. My awareness of that primitive theology coursed through my body, electrifying my senses. It has been my beacon ever since.

It was Mark Twain who declared about the Bible: "It has noble poetry in it, and some clever fables, and some blood-drenched history, and some good morals." And then he added that it has "a wealth of obscenity, and upwards of a thousand lies." The author, a Presbyterian, was describing the Bible for its greatest strength—its realism about human life and vanities.

The fundamentalists don't realize that it's not the best-selling book in history because people are stuck on the spectacles. These miracles are cartoons and, yes, children and adults enjoy animation. But what really animates the scriptural narrative, like any enduring literature or media, is the unending, undistilled flow of nonsupernatural events: illicit sexual encounters, palace intrigue, double-crossings, family dysfunction, homicides, and territorial wars.

Keep your cataclysms; I'm going with plain old, skewed human behavior. And that behavior includes the reality that the brilliant people who inscribed such important and revered stories were doing their best writing when they illustrated how we humans have very complicated personal relationships with the God we turn to when we are in trouble.

Of course it's the longest-running literature on Earth! Anything this true-to-life would sell with gusto. Those overzealous preachers want to grab you with the parting seas, the people rising from the dead (and this didn't just happen with Jesus), the manna falling from heaven, or the rivers turning into blood. I've noticed, however, that the largest crowds seem to gather in church or synagogue (or via television) when one of those ministers offers a remorseful, teary sermon asking forgiveness for having "fallen into weakness" through pilfering the donation box, lust, adultery, or fondling someone's child.

A lot of people looking for a belief system simply don't realize that twisted and improbable behavior is a huge layer of scripture. It contains flashes of acerbic wit, instances of mind-bending deceptions, and moments of incomprehensible cruelty. Rather than putting you off, this edifying aspect of the old writ should make it all the more accessible and more believable. These flashes of human vulnerability and imperfection should help you to reflect on your own attributes. They will enlighten you about what we human beings can and do inflict upon each other.

Some folks in the Bible are likable, others are insufferable; they all sweat, copulate, make plans, doubt God, look for food, distract their bosses, abide by civil regulations, pay taxes, relocate from time to time, discipline their children, put up with condescending neighbors, suffer through wars, and bury their dead. They spend a lot less time praying to their gods than they do paying their debtors. They do all of this with the same cyclical bursts of energy, bouts of laziness, enthusiasm, skepticism, bravado, fear, humiliation, and skittishness that attend our own lives.

Moses had a physical handicap—he stuttered and turned over the public speaking portion of his civil rights campaign to his brother, Aaron. Rachel was an intermittent kleptomaniac known to remove things from other people's tents. Saul, the first king of Israel, suffered from chemical depression and chronic jealous rage: He once threw a spear at the young David because the teenager was playing the harp in the palace and it irritated the king.

A woman named Tamar (one of four ancestors of Jesus) fought back against sexual harassment and publicly shamed her assailant, Judah, who was one of the twelve sons of Jacob and from whose name is derived the term, "Jew."

The Bible is a library of stories about human flaws written by human hands and all intended to document the perpetual, necessary, and informative mortal encounter with both demons and angels. It's what we theologize about on Saturdays and Sundays but the working material actually unfolds Monday through Friday.

Everyone naturally associates Noah with the apocalyptic flood. In fact, Noah had a serious problem with alcoholism and the latter part of his life was scandalous and an embarrassment to his three sons. The message from Ephesians in the New Testament would have evaded the old man: "Fathers, do not exasperate your children."

Sometime after the waters had receded, Noah took up wine making. The Bible tells us: "Noah, a man of the soil, proceeded to plant a vineyard." Of course, that's fine and, in and by itself, not problematic. But the story doesn't stop there:

> He drank of the wine and became drunk, and uncovered himself inside his tent. Ham, the father of Canaan, saw the nakedness of his father, and told his two brothers outside.

So Noah of the Bible was discovered lolling around his shanty, inebriated and exposed. How many of us have made a painful discovery of or about a parent? As a clergyman, I cannot count how many anguished children, of all ages, have come to me in tears, fright, and exasperation: A parent was a drunk, an embezzler, a compulsive gambler, an impossible debtor, a serial adulterer, or a person given to physically abuse members of his or her family.

Confronted with these kinds of crises, we are coiled in an agonizing mixture of anger, guilt, helplessness, and social humiliation. We have joined Al-Anon, the National Recovery Association (violence against women), Safe Horizon (child abuse), After Silence (post-rape), or Psych Central (emotional abuse). There are, thankfully, innumerable caring outreach centers for recovering substance users, rehabilitating sexual addicts, and for prisoners who've done their time and are reentering society. Mercifully, there are community organizations that rescue and protect children recuperating from physical, emotional, and mental cruelty.

The fact of the matter is that there is no local, state, or national support agency that would not have experienced a long line of subscribers from the ranks of "Bible heroes." There is much more distress in "The Good Book" than there is divinity.

Imagine the cringing feelings of Noah's three sons in the subsequent sentences of this imbibing/exposure episode:

And Shem and Japheth [Noah's two other sons] *took a garment, laid it upon both their shoulders, and walked backwards and covered the nakedness of their father. And their faces were backward and they saw not their father's nakedness.*

Then, when Noah opened his drowsy eyes, he returned the favor by castigating the son who found him strung out and then told the other brothers about it: "Cursed be Canaan," blasted the old drunkard, referring to Ham's son. "A servant of servants shall he be unto his brethren."

Good boys, pathetic father. The Bible is telling it like it is here, and this is the Bible I believe in.

There is really no end to this revealing and trenchant aspect of the ongoing scriptural literature. I call it the chronicle of brilliant madness: At one point, Christ yelled irrationally at a fig tree for not bearing figs off-season. The great Isaiah, who pleaded that "nation shall not lift up sword against nation," also experienced an episode of running around barefoot and naked. Ezekiel, the haunting poet of "the valley of dry bones," lay down on his side for a marathon 390 days and ate human excrement.

We have already examined Sarah's indefensible and outlandish banishment of Hagar and her child Ishmael to die off in the desert. And what of the First Family of dysfunction—Adam and Eve? Eve had an obvious eating disorder as she simply could not resist the sugary, forbidden fruit of the garden. She and her mate Adam raised two sons in their "paradise" digs—only to suffer the ultimate domestic horror when one son, Cain, knifed his brother Abel to death.

Solomon, who was notoriously promiscuous, was attributed to have had some 1,000 sexual partners. He was both a carnal addict and an astonishing poet of human desire. In "The Song of Songs," one of the later wisdom books in the Old Testament, Solomon fancifully composed:

Behold thou art fair, my love . . . thou hast doves' eyes within thy locks. Thy hair is as a flock of goats . . . thy teeth are like a flock of sheep that are even shorn . . . thy lips are like a thread of scarlet.

Then he wrote:

Thy two breasts are like two young roes that are twins, which feed among the lilies.

Then he wrote:

Thou hast ravished my heart, my sister, my spouse! How much better is thy love than wine! And the smell of thine ointments than all spices!

Solomon is traditionally cited by religious academics for his incomparable wisdom as a judge and arbiter. And there can be no doubt about the vast intellect and profound genius of this ancient, nimble, and passionate king who predated the designation, "Renaissance man." He loved life, clout, and women. He performed no divine miracles and all of his exploits are lined with flaws, yearnings, improprieties, and immortal creative works. His life was a white-hot flame of managed dysfunction and breakthrough leadership.

With bacchanalian flare, he waxed unapologetically about sex—pure physical love, unchaste adoration, and, in "The Song of Songs," about a navel that he likened to "a round goblet." He compared his subject's breasts to grapes, to "clusters of the vine," and he equated "the smell of thy nose" to "apples." In his "Song," he added:

And the roof of thy mouth [is] like the best wine that goeth down sweetly for my beloved, causing the lips of those that are asleep to speak.

And yet, this is the chief magistrate who expertly designed and constructed the stunning Holy Temple of Jerusalem—on the backs of his subjects. His Judean constituents excoriated him for overtaxing them mercilessly in the process, while he enjoyed a sinfully lavish lifestyle.

Our public figures inspire us with their charismas in direct proportion to how they exasperate us with their egos. But we are drawn to them just as we drawn to the glowing heat of the fire.

And then there was Solomon's father, David—cloaked in Christian Messianism and revered as a powerfully talented musician and psalmist. Having survived Saul's flung spear, he grew into an acutely dysfunctional sovereign himself. He was one of the most criminally sexual deviants in the history of monarchs. Not only did he freely fornicate, he literally arranged to have a lover's husband's killed off to protect his pleasures. As one Christian theologian has written about this incident, "In the whole of the Old Testament literature, there is no chapter more tragic or full of solemn and searching warning than this."

The Bible tells us that David, who had trouble sleeping, was walking on the roof of his palatial estate one early evening and noticed an exquisite woman sunbathing across the way. This was the famous Bathsheba, a visiting foreign queen. It is not unlikely that the shapely royal was seductively sprawled out at that very moment quite on purpose. Upon noticing and lusting over her, David immediately had some of his attendants get the low-down on this woman. Yes, this was Bathsheba. Married. Wife of a gallant Hittite hero named Uriah.

"Go get her for me."

This tawdry tale can be found in the Second Book of Samuel. Yes, it exists in the same contiguous sacred scroll as the Ten Commandments and the Resurrection.

And David sent messengers, and took her, and she came in unto him, and he lay with her.

The Bible then cuts to the chase:

And the woman conceived and sent and told David, I am with child.

Not to worry, this was hardly going to be a deterrent for David the King. He summarily wrote out some military orders dispatching the woman's husband, Uriah—a skilled and admired soldier—into a hopeless battle that was ongoing for the Judean armies. David was so depraved here that he even assigned one of his lieutenants to make certain that Uriah would be positioned in the most impossibly dangerous zone during the hostilities. Uriah was killed—or, if you will, murdered by the fabled king and musician who also gave us the soaring and elegiac Psalm 23:

The Lord is my shepherd; I shall not want.
He makes me lie down in green pastures.
He leads me beside still waters.
He restores my soul.
He leads me in the paths of righteousness for his name's sake.
Even though I walk through the valley of the shadow of death,
I will fear no evil,
For you are with me;
Your rod and your staff,
They comfort me . . .

What do you say about such a man, who was the living contradiction of the most extreme passions and differing needs known to people—especially people vaulted into history by these spiritual paradoxes? Totally obsessed with conquering women, able to send another man to a painful death under the most obscene and contrived circumstances, yet perhaps the greatest lyricist of all time? David slew Goliath but never slew his own demons.

In our own time, we have seen many compelling leaders, political and celebrity, who captured our hearts and imagination. But whether through theft, sexually deviant misconduct, or other unfathomable behaviors they fell from that place of grace. Is public brilliance somehow linked to private hyper-vanity? Are great men and women not great in tandem with their manias? Is poetry not the transcript of inner turmoil?

Whatever the answers are to these questions, the Bible is working for me when it is putting the inquiries out there. Certainly it is a more credible document when, as my long-ago mentor Philip Mendelsohn told me, "The heroes stick in our guts because they are real."

Bathsheba was not totally innocent in the story above. She clearly wooed the man in the first place with her physical charms and guile. The Bible declares that after learning her husband was dead, she did mourn for him. We don't know if David revealed his complicity in Uriah's killing—one tends to doubt he did. The story ends with the following straightforward dispatch:

> *And when the mourning was past, David sent and fetched her to his house. She became his wife and bore him a son.*

Imperial power and sexual politics surely played roles here; in Jerusalem in those days, a woman did not necessarily have the ability to deny David the King. It is the same crude cycle that still prevails today with any number of politicians and/or celebrities. I gratefully note the biblical writer's final sentence in that episode: "But the thing that David had done displeased the Lord."

I am much more inclined to contemplate divine judgment expressed in such quiet reflection than via a series of flamboyant and supernatural gestures of theatrical annoyance.

Give me the fingerprints of real souls, not the ephemeral trails of supposed saints. Give me an indignant Jesus, who, according to Matthew, let certain theologians he disliked suffer his spleen: "You serpents, you brood of vipers, how shall you escape the sentence of hell?" And then in Luke, when he dumped on the legal profession (as we are all-too-often inclined to do): "Woe to you lawyers! For you have taken away the key of knowledge."

The Bible succeeds when it's brazenly candid, deliciously frank, and when it makes me feel that I can be a good person without having to be perfect. I don't have to be angelic to learn a lot from these angels.

The Bible endures because its characters are, for the most part, capable of doing inscrutable things—like human beings always have been. Witness the world's one hundred ongoing wars, our modern penal crisis, our suburban, heavy-duty pharmaceutical cubicles euphemistically termed "medicine cabinets," and our intermittent mass school shootings. Note the interminable bloodletting of the Holy Land, the very soil of heaven on Earth that can't even sustain its own peaceful Jerusalem.

Let's face it: You don't witness a thunderbolt striking down a mob of nonbelievers every day but you do observe a domestic murder or a child-snatching almost daily on cable television or over your YouTube feed. There comes a time, somewhere between the innocence of childhood and the maturity of being a grown-up, when you realize the story of Noah and the Flood was not a charming parable. It was a wanton, global liquidation executed by a spoiled deity who didn't like his toys and decided to just wash them away and get new ones. Here's the divine dysfunction that unfolded into the DNA of two Testaments—and into the world ever since. The Bible serves to remind us that there has always been evil and wickedness. The problem is that we now live in an epoch of nonstop cyber and media delivery of the evil and thereby are hypnotized into believing that it's something new.

Let us return to the indomitably authentic David. Like all predatory males, there came a time when he was reduced by age and feebleness and a worn-out virility. The Bible is hardly ever more reliable as it tells about the pathetic old king at the end of his life:

> *Now King David was old, advanced in age; and they covered him with clothes, but he could not keep warm. So his servants said to him, "Let them seek a young virgin for my lord the king, and let her attend the king and become his nurse; and let her lie in your bosom, that my lord the king may keep warm."*

Indeed, a maiden named Abishag was discovered after a nationwide search for the best, most fetching candidate for the job. She was, in the Bible's words, "a comely young woman." They delivered her to the quivering and wrinkled liege, now a sliver of his championship self under a heap of blankets. She dutifully got into bed with him.

> *The woman was very beautiful; she took care of the king and waited on him, but the king had no sexual relations with her.*

How ironic, and how true to life, that it was this same David who had written in the Book of Psalms: "Do not cast me away when I am old; do not forsake me when my strength is gone." Even David knew the miracles would not last forever.

Chapter Eleven

FROM INSECURITY TO INTERMARRIAGE

"Can two walk together, unless they have agreed?"
—The Hebrew Scripture

W HO AND WHAT COME to mind when you think about Moses?

❖ Chief rabbi and teacher in Hebrew history?

❖ Performer of deific miracles?

❖ Paternal and legislative icon for all three Western faiths?

❖ Biblical foil for Pharaoh?

❖ Liberator and leader of the world's first freedom march?

How about a man who was intermarried—twice! Moses was first wedded to Zipporah, who was a daughter of the Midianite high priest, Jethro. The decidedly non-Jewish woman was the lawgiver's lover and partner during most of the years of wandering in the Sinai desert. We have already pointed to the exceptionally warm and nurturing role Jethro played as a father figure in the life of Moses.

Scripture leaves us wondering how and when Zipporah parted from Moses but she evidently did not survive the wilderness journey. This mystery, however, does not detract from the rabbinic enthusiasm recorded for this formidable pagan woman who pursued, protected, and captivated Moses.

A modern scholar named Tamar Kadari has created a profile for the woman who gave Moses his two sons. Scanning rabbinic literature, with its unique, balanced cadence of adoration and skepticism about the ancient heroes, Kadari gets a sense of Zipporah by listening to the scholarly music. Kadari declares that the rabbinic tradition is very upbeat about Zipporah. The old sages, stroking their beards, looking to turn a peripheral female character into a three-dimensional partner for the greatest rabbi of all time, played fast and loose with the text, which they massaged for their creative purposes. They intuited her thorny self-awareness and detected the lingering sadness of her life. They made a brilliant, confident woman out of someone who might have been dismissed in today's derisive jargon as a *shiksa* (a contemptible Yiddish term still widely used to describe a non-Jewish woman). More than anything else, however, they liked this non-Hebrew woman who Moses wedded. Kadari writes:

> "The Rabbis ascribe many traits to Zipporah, whom they considered as differing from other women, in a positive sense, in both appearance and deed. A beautiful woman, she had received a special blessing that her comeliness would last her into old age. She is also described as a practical woman capable of taking action at the right moment."

So it appears that Zipporah was yet another spiritual pragmatist. What were some of her notable actions? Why did the ancient Jewish spiritual authorities bend over backward to approve of Zipporah when so many contemporary rabbinic agencies stridently disapprove of intermarriage?

The answer: This resourceful woman, whose Hebrew name means "sparrow" or "the little bird," was (as we shall see) simply too spiritually nimble and too passionate about her loved ones to be dismissed just because she wasn't Jewish. It all began at a desert well—one of the more often used, wide-open settings employed by the biblical writers. (Most of the faith stories are set against the universalistic intersections of sand and water.)

In fact, Moses arrived at this well after fleeing alone and in terror from Egyptian justice. In an act of impulsive rage, he had suddenly slain an Egyptian taskmaster who was pummeling a helpless Hebrew slave. The incident is clearly written in the Bible. Moses, born a Hebrew, had circumstantially grown up in Pharaoh's household but the narrative suggests that he was always ambivalent about his identity. Sometimes, we find out who we really are when we witness something ruthlessly offensive and thereby defining. Thankfully, not all of us react by killing somebody. Moses may have discovered his Hebrew DNA, but he also realized he was now in serious legal trouble—regardless of his palace connections.

Now the fugitive, who was thirsty, desperate, and lonely, came upon this desert crossing where people gathered to collect water from a community well. The seven daughters of Jethro were drawing water for themselves and for their sheep. They noticed the sunburned, parched stranger who wandered in. Zipporah definitely noticed.

Before any flirting could begin, a disturbing intrusion occurred: A crew of wilderness thugs pounced upon the women and tried to extract their filled troughs. Moses valiantly fought these bandits off and proceeded to water the women's sheep. The grateful lasses returned to their father's tent and described the event to Jethro.

Jethro was surprised the girls had returned so quickly from the well. They reported:

An Egyptian man rescued us from the shepherds; he even drew water for us and watered the flock.

"Where is he, then?" The High Priest was mortified at this breach of desert hospitality. Moreover, with seven unmarried daughters, he saw other possibilities. The women were ashamed as Jethro continued the upbraiding.

Why did you leave the man? Go back, find him, and ask him in to break bread.

And so it was that the Hebrew/Egyptian hero was brought to the home of the Midianite priest and his family. Moses stayed on and was betrothed to Zipporah, and she eventually gave birth to their sons, Gershom and Eliezer. Like some 65 percent of marriages in America today involving a Jewish partner, this was an interfaith situation, a merger of customs and behaviors, replete with its challenges and opportunities. It was a paradigm of the wandering demographic that is now the map of our national religious culture.

I mention this historical fact about Moses to parents who become outraged or hostile when a child of theirs brings someone home, someone beloved, who happens to be of a different heritage. I tell them that Moses married out of the faith (twice) but nonetheless went on to a successful and high profile career in the Jewish nonprofit sector. He is eternally revered by the community as a) the premier sage of all time and b) the only human being who has ever spoken with God directly and without an intercessor.

As in many blended family situations today, it was the "non-Jewish partner" who was proactive regarding the appropriate observances and rituals. Moses was indifferent to the Abrahamic procedural of circumcision for his sons. This created a near-fatal moment between Moses and God. In fact, the Bible tells us that while Moses and Zipporah and the family were fighting the blistering heat and sand storms en route back to Egypt, God became homicidal just as Moses sought some lodging one evening.

> *And it came to pass by the way in the inn, that the Lord met him and sought to kill him.*

That's right: God was going to terminate Moses because his two boys hadn't been circumcised. Enter Zipporah to save the day. With alacrity and swiftness, she "took a sharp stone and cut off the foreskin of her son." Then the Bible gets quite personal about the tension between Zipporah and her husband—even as what she suddenly did saved Moses from being slain by the Almighty. Referring to her son's foreskin:

> *She cast it at Moses's feet and said, "Surely a bloody husband art thou, because of the circumcision."*

It doesn't get much blunter than that in most any literature. And yes, this is the Bible I can believe in. I'm not going to speculate about the medical and sanitary conditions that did or did not exist during this painfully roughshod procedure out in the open. Worse things happen every day in American hospitals: botched or incorrect surgeries, misallocated medications, preferential treatments. What intrigues me in our story is the boldness of the woman set against the laxness of the man.

Zipporah was hardly a submissive, dutiful wife who hid behind the persona of her well-known husband. Maybe it was her love for him (which transcended the faith differences) that propelled her to step in, do the circumcision, and cool off God's temper. Perhaps she did it to spare her young sons the anguish of losing their father. Zipporah was clearly not happy with Moses, tossing the foreskin at his sandals and describing him as "a bloody husband"—a burst of intimate ferocity more intelligible to us readers than any deity-driven eruption of a mountain in the biblical chronicles.

"A bloody husband?" Matthew Henry, an eighteenth century Christian commentator wrote: "The words are clearly a reproach; and the gist of the reproach seems to be that Moses was a husband who cost her dearly, causing the blood of her sons to be shed in order to keep up a national usage which she regarded as barbarous." There are plenty of modern Jews who have their reservations about circumcision. This little domestic tempest in the Torah is very much a contemporary and recurring health and ethical debate ongoing in the general community.

A marriage where there exists strain and disagreement? Two parents struggling ideologically over religious rites and about how or how not to please God? Are these not two classic conditions characteristic of real-life family tensions? I find this kind of conflict in the Bible to be of much greater merit than putting together two saintly spouses who aren't prone to any original thinking and just slumber in their obeisance to divine indulgence. And I love that Zipporah is neither Jewish nor compliant and that her relationship to her superstar Hebrew husband is fodder for some of the most unfettered acclamation in all the Jewish texts.

Before people bring their creeds to a marriage, they bring their characters. Love, human desire, and soulful partnerships are not underwritten by religious criteria. I've worked with two people who were both Jewish and completely unqualified to be married to each other. Some folks are not equipped to be married to anyone. I've certainly interacted with blended couples—when both parties were uniquely suited to one another, they needed each other, and the burden of bringing their two faith traditions to the situation actually strengthened their listening and learning skills in favor of the relationship.

If you can toil through and find common ground on theology, then you likely will have an advantage in mastering your taxes, grocery lists, and checkbook. I'm not saying people of the same faith should not consider marrying nor am I suggesting that intermarriage does not present special challenges and burdens. It would also be downright disingenuous for anyone to even imply that scriptural text is not filled with grim injunctions against intermarriage—even while it is filled with the narratives of polygamists ranging from Solomon to Mohammed.

Indeed, the Muslim Prophet sired scores of children from many wives. His indomitable original wife, an international caravan entrepreneur and divorcée named Khadija, fifteen years his senior, converted to Islam. Both Abraham and Sarah, the founding parents of Judaism, were born as pagans who, as elders, elected to their ultimate faith. Samson, the heavyweight champion of the Jews with jaw-dropping strength but a weakness for alcohol, had a wandering eye that transcended his faith community. Note this passage from Judges:

> And Samson went down to Timnath, and saw a woman in Timnath of the daughters of the Philistines.

Suffice it to say that Samson got the girl, even though his parents went ballistic over his choice:

> Then his father and his mother said unto him, "Is there not a woman among the daughters of thy brethren, or among all my people, that thou goest to take a wife of the uncircumcised Philistines?" And Samson said unto his father, "Get her for me; for she pleaseth me well."

So when it comes to blended relationships as conveyed in the holy writ, we can either go tribal, (which is often the toxic root of today's religiously driven terrorism) or we can go with tolerant human nature. We can choose inclusiveness over insecurity.

Love is indifferent to political history, and it disdains human bigotry. Love is also colorblind; just look in the Bible—again at Moses.

After Zipporah was gone, Moses remarried. His new wife was, again, not a Hebrew. She was black; the Bible refers to her cryptically as "the Ethiopian woman." Sadly, this woman is never given a name in the text—there is a kind of painful revelation in her eternal anonymity. Moses surely called out to her by name and undoubtedly knew her skin, her breath, and the rustle of her coal-dark hair as it flew in the dry wind. His siblings, Miriam and Aaron, definitively called out to their sister-in-law with racial epithets and unseemly sentiments:

And Miriam and Aaron spoke against Moses because of the Ethiopian woman whom he had married; for he had married an Ethiopian woman.

The obvious racial liberty in the marriage of their brother to the Ethiopian made the two leader-siblings anxious. Aaron was the chief priest of Israel and Miriam was the nation's resident musician. But looking upon their brother's dark-skinned second wife, these two prelates simply disintegrated into two covetous and bitter siblings. They blurted out in jealous rebuke: "Has the Lord spoken only to Moses? Hasn't he spoken to us too?"

In other words, is Moses so special that he can do whatever he wants, including falling in love with a black woman? In case anyone with prejudicial tendencies shares in this plainly expressed outburst of racialism on the siblings' part, God would sharply differ; the verse above ends with the phrase, "And the Lord heard it." The Bible continues:

At once the LORD said to Moses, Aaron, and Miriam, "Come out to the tent of meeting, all three of you." So the three of them went out. Then the LORD descended in the pillar of cloud and stood at the entrance of the Tabernacle. "Aaron and Miriam!" he called, and they stepped forward.

It's hard not to get the sense that the Lord's mood was unfavorable. In short, after reminding Aaron and Miriam that Moses enjoys divine approval (and, by implication, can marry whomever he chooses), the following happens:

The wrath of the Lord flared against them . . . The cloud departed from above the Tent, and behold, Miriam was afflicted with leprosy. Aaron said to Moses, "Please, master, do not put sin upon us for acting foolishly and for sinning. Let her not be like the dead, which comes out of his mother's womb with half his flesh consumed!"

Here's an instance when the supernatural goings-on in scripture are working for me. The moral implication of the story is clear and, to paraphrase Dr. Martin Luther King, Jr., it bends toward justice. God literally calls two kinfolk out because they were judgmental and discriminatory in gossiping about their brother's choice of a mate. It didn't help, either, that their social elitism turned them into two adult brats who suddenly resented Moses's power and prestige.

Does this refute the presence of all the severely prohibitive legislation in the Bible about mixed marriage? No, but it sure says a great deal about the ebb and flow of life and circumstances and about how attitudes evolve, even within the library of religion. Remember: There are stringent, even threatening edicts against homosexual relationships in the Bible as well.

So do we then simply dispense with the compelling love story, examined earlier, involving Jonathan and David? One finds forbidding laws over here, redemptive stories over there—all within the seal of scripture. So what is the last word on these things, these passions, and these authentic human dramas? Who's to say what's right?

Perhaps the answer came a long time ago, from Moses himself—at the very moment his brother Aaron was fear-stricken and his sister found herself throbbing and stinging from both the pain and shame of leprosy. Even though he, Moses, was the one being covetously trashed and his wife was being racially marginalized, he still found it within his heart to plead for healing:

> *Moses cried out to the Lord, saying, "I beseech you, God, please cure her."*

The punishment was stayed; Miriam was healed after seven days. That was long enough for everyone in the camp to hear that no one is above the natural law of tolerance and that God Almighty will not suffer the indignity of human prejudice in the category of love.

Early in 2015, a review appeared in the *Huffington Post* about a book entitled *Strange Wives: The Paradox of Biblical Intermarriage*. It was written by the late Stanley Ned Rosenbaum, with help from Rabbi Allen Secher. Professor Rosenbaum was a premier biblical scholar who was married to a Catholic woman and who devoted assiduous research into the question of ancient intermarriage. In the book, Rosenbaum and Secher wrote: "Tradition has forgotten, if it ever knew, how religiously diverse early Israel was."

The reviewer, Susan Katz Miller, summarized the work of these two inclusive and substantive Jewish thinkers:

"The authors document marriages of Israelites with Ammonites, Amalekites, Moabites, Midianites, Samaritans, Canaanites, Amorites, Hittites, Egyptians, and Babylonians. The women who married into the tribes of Israel continued to worship their own fertility gods even after marriage, and early Israelite farmers continued to appeal to fertility gods to bless their crops, and saw their God as competing with, incorporating, subsuming, and possibly even (inter)marrying other local gods."

All you have to do is thumb through the pages of the Hebrew scripture and, like a canonical phonebook, discover the endless names of nomads, planters, oracles, soothsayers, ecclesiastics, warriors, well-diggers, cartographers, money-changers, slave-drivers, stargazers, camel drivers, teachers, and census-takers who wove their lives into those of the Hebrew and Judean ancestors of our faith systems.

It all began the day the Hebrew slaves were liberated from Egypt. The Bible specifically refers to "a mixed multitude" that escaped under the aegis of Moses. In other words, all kinds of ethnic bondsmen and bondswomen—black, brown, bronzed, multiracial—broke out of prison on that historic occasion. The sinister Pharaonic net of slavery extended across the crescent of the Near East; there was certainly one Ethiopian woman in the throng who eventually got the personal attention of Moses. The multifarious, vibrant, fluid, interlinking, biblical world that we calcify in our religious insecurities was actually a "cultural caravansary"— as phrased by Susan Katz Miller. The people in that world, from Ruth to David to Esther, regularly intermarried.

In the Jewish community, particularly, there is a lot of hand wringing about the advancing number of coreligionists marrying Christians. It's an issue that draws a fretful, voluble response, many forbidding demographic charts revealed at community seminars and published in newspapers, along with intermittent pronouncements of demographic doom. Over the years, I have heard the escalating rate of intermarriage among Jews likened to a "spiritual Holocaust." It's hard not to regret such a declaration.

Beyond the attendant trivialization of the mass extermination of six million Jewish people (including 1.5 million children) carried out by the Nazis and their willing accomplices across Europe, the comparison is feckless. Those innocent victims of the greatest genocide in world history were gassed, shot, hung, drowned, asphyxiated, starved to death, burned, or buried alive. In short, they were murdered. The people we are talking about in this free America are getting married. Hundreds of thousands of the accumulated dead in Europe were Christians who were married to Jews, or whose parents or grandparents had incidentally been Jewish or part-Jewish, or who were biologically and randomly linked to the "racial contamination" the Nazis connected to the Jews because of, say, some distant great-uncle who had once set foot in a synagogue and uttered a Hebrew devotion.

I'm not going to let Nazi ideology turn into an instrument of my sensitivities—and responsibilities—to people in this society who love each other. I'm not going to regard their commitment to one another as a threat. I'm going to regard it as an opportunity. I can't respond to what they feel for each other as something alarming on a statistical chart. It is much more a reflection of something wonderful happening in the human heart.

We clergy need to become a part of the solution, not part of the problem.

When Jewish parents come to me, trembling with guilt and a sense of failure, telling me their son or daughter wants to marry a non-Jew, I do acknowledge their sentiments. I don't dismiss their anguish just as I hardly diminish the tyranny of the number six million. I know that between 1933 and 1945, one of every three Jews on this planet was vaporized. The cultural Jewish dominion of Poland, many centuries running, with its grand Torah academies and breathtakingly magnificent synagogues and its Talmudic dignity—replete with joyous music and heartrending liturgical poetry—were all destroyed (with three million human beings) in a few brutish years. Romanian Jewish grandmothers were slaughtered in their own kitchens, Czech Jewish students lynched, French Jewish babies loaded up in sealed boxcars and shipped from Paris to Auschwitz for industrial extermination, and Dutch Jewish girls raped until dead in SS barracks. From Portugal to Greece, from Finland to Italy, Jewish blood drenched the earth and Jewish ashes clouded the skies.

In the most vile and extreme sense, Jewish persons were excluded, legally and terminally, from mixing in with any other kinds of persons. This hate, divide-and-kill national policy was also pitilessly applied to an additional six million people—the Roma (gypsies), homosexuals, Jehovah's Witnesses, the physically and mentally handicapped, Soviet prisoners-of-war, innumerable Catholic priests who spoke out against the brutality aimed at "the people of Abraham," all Christians who allegedly hid Jews, Christians who were suspected of having sexual relations with Jews, and sundry critics, progressives, and "undesirables."

Now, a short seven decades later, on an American continent tending toward inclusivism, knowing how Jewish (and other) kids had no hope and no future, I'm supposed to submit to further social segregation? I'm expected to acquiesce to the policing of human love? That is not what the personal history of Moses suggests to me. It's not what I hear in the emotionally tinted psalms of David or what I discern from the courageous journey of Ruth.

Ruth, a Moabite widow, an ancestor of Jesus, loved Boaz—a Jewish landowner depicted in the scriptural volume named for this noble and passionate woman. Ruth dwelled with her mother-in-law, Naomi, who had also been widowed. Boaz was generous to both women with his gifts of grain and seasonal work at the Jewish harvests. Naomi encouraged her Moabite daughter-in-law to travel to Israel and allow Boaz to court her. Ruth famously answered: "Wherever you go, there I will go." Ruth and Boaz wed; yet another hallmark blended marriage canonized in scripture.

And Ruth's mantra is, thankfully, the American story—just seventy years after 1945. Our children can, for the most part, go wherever they wish to go: universities, corporations, high political office, and into the arms of any lover who is the right one in the category of the heart.

I talk with agitated Jewish parents who decry their new interfaith situation and who ask me, "Why did this happen?" I tell them, "Why? Because we have succeeded. We have graduated from the concentration camps to the courtyards of law and commerce and education without distinctions, quotas, and legal barriers based upon creed. We have emerged from the ghettos into mainstream society and our children can mix with, befriend, and romance an unlimited new range of people. We have replaced fear with love."

I ask them to remember how history and its duplicitous ally, religion, have been driving people apart for centuries. I tell them love is not a liturgy; it is a language. And when people are talking the same language, then that's when all the rest of us have a prayer.

Chapter Twelve

"THE KING SHALL NOT HAVE TOO MANY HORSES"

DEEP WITHIN THE LIBYAN section of the Sahara Desert, underneath a merciless sun, there is a fabled cavern known as the Cave of Swimmers. The grotto is tucked away among the jagged mountains of the Gilf Kebir plateau. A large number of *wadis* infiltrate the plateau—the region is visually stunning, mysterious, and stark with its solar-scarred secrets and haunting shadows, physically treacherous, and impossibly magnetic for explorers and sightseers.

The Cave of Swimmers, with its Neolithic pictographs (dating back to the New Stone Age some 10,000 years ago), engraved rock art, and old ghosts, is prominently featured in the 1996 motion picture, *The English Patient*, starring Ralph Fiennes and Kristin Scott Thomas. They play war-crossed, illicit lovers who wind up seeking shelter in the Cave. The woman has been dangerously injured and the man must leave her alone, with a flickering flashlight, in order to venture out and seek help. She will not survive his absence and eventually dies in the darkness.

Before his departure, she makes a statement that has never left me. She is the British wife of a National Geographic mapmaker; he is a Hungarian aristocrat who was also attached to the cartographic team exploring the area for the most peaceful, scientific purposes. The Nazis were advancing in North Africa and the desert dunes and slopes were being converted into an expansive, blistering battlefield.

The woman asks her lover about why there are so many flags, which just divide people.

This guttural plea, this grievance against certain freedom killing, happiness-pulling nations and institutions of our world, these organisms of territoriality and domination and manipulation, remains resonant for me. What is the expediency of all these flags, the global jurisdictions, the national officialdoms, the religious regimes, if they in fact amount to nothing more than a series of insecure, power-driven, divisive, and repressive administrations that simply suffocate the life out of human freedom?

World War II was an Armageddon that took the lives of fifty-nine million people. Many of the flags that flapped in ghastly battles do not even exist anymore. The vast majority of these flags' victims were civilians— schoolchildren, parents, and townspeople—innocent souls swept into the inferno by opposing military alliances in an atomic rush to hell.

Granted, the war was a crucial, do-or-die struggle against the genocidal elitism of the German-Japanese Axis on the part of the resolutely determined forces of the Anglo-American led Allies. I am not questioning the necessity or the glory of what the Allies accomplished. Some wars must be fought. However, all existing or potential tyrants need to be restrained; this decreases the possibility of wars. Where is this notion found? It is inscribed early in scripture, almost hidden in the Book of Deuteronomy.

When you come into the land that God gives you . . . and say, I will set a king over me, like all the nations about me . . . the King shall not have too many horses, nor cause the people to return to Egypt.

". . . cause the people to return to Egypt." Let's examine this peculiar closing phrase first.

Yes, besides the concern that a royal could get arrogant and despotic if conferred too many hooves and chariots, there is yet another burst of spiritual pragmatism revealed here. If there are a lot of horses and wheels available to seize from the king's court, and things aren't going so well for the always cantankerous Hebrews in their new land, well then, somebody might be tempted to pull off a flight back to Egypt. There was always a fifth column during the desert trek to the Promised Land that complained and whined about the heat, the lack of water, and the alleged haughtiness of Moses. The leader had to quell two serious rebellions while in transit. Yes, there were some folks who became nostalgic for Egypt where at least they were fed, had a routine, and didn't suffer the occasional enraged outbursts of that God for whom Moses worked.

So an underlying, practical reason for keeping the number of horses down in the new province was to, frankly, lower the availability of escape vehicles. This obscure proclamation in the Old Testament, besides construing imperial egos so intuitively, is a worthwhile gem highly worth believing in.

There is recognition in the early Bible that the Israelites would pine for a king once they had settled in Israel and established themselves among the family of nations. Why? Because all the other countries around them had kings. Now, a king is not necessarily the same thing as an elected president or a prime minister, but the intent is the same: to establish a chief who is able to lead but not lose touch with the people being led. Scripture's language here is rustic, perhaps, but telling nonetheless: "The king shall not have too many horses." (Read: too many luxury vehicles and/or armored carriers).

It's fair to say the notions of "limited government" and "checks and balances" are not recent manifestations; they're actually 3,000 years old and come straight out of Deuteronomy. I'm struck by the old-fashioned insight here. A ruler with too many horses or limousines or airplanes is a ruler at risk of forgetting who he (or she) is or isn't. No miracles here, just wisdom and logicality packed into this insightful assertion about dominant men (and women) and realism. I'm hoping the increasingly vocal and theologically righteous segment of our national political hierarchy is actually reading this lesser-known section of the Bible. It may not have a lot of fire and brimstone but it sure could save us all from the sanctimonious rhetoric that is choking our country into deadlock in the category of social justice.

The distinguished contemporary biblical critic, Professor Richard Elliott Friedman, has written in his *Commentary on the Torah* about this passage. He praises the idea that kings should be restricted from the indulgence of too much might. He makes the point that a king (or any ruler) with too many vehicles and armaments creates a privileged and powerful upper class requiring serfs and such underlings to service them. This also results in an unfair social system and the danger of insurrection.

It appears this grounded, nonsupernatural segment of scripture was way ahead of our own times when it recognized the ignominy of "the 1 percent" dominating the "99 percent." It is serious, judicious business implying much more than the constant patronizing implemented by the politicians who blather that "Wall Street is as important as Main Street."

The biblical king is also warned "not to take too many wives for himself." Not only that, the king is directed "not to take too much gold and silver for himself" and to keep not one, but two sets of holy books around the palace. It turns out there is an entirely accessible tier of scripture that is more interested in democracy than in demagoguery. And this is a piece of religious literature I can embrace; all it's trying to do is improve human behavior—especially the behavior of folks who are in positions of power from which they can influence our daily lives.

The scripture is not demanding that the king not have horses. It is simply reprimanding him not to have *too many* horses. Maybe the king had too many horses with which to play. The Bible is talking common sense here and we can see its cogent wisdom in the revelations of today's headlines.

For the person in these perplexing times who doesn't know what to believe, I again submit that there is a fulfilling layer of the scriptural library that does service one's need to access useful and edifying ideas. I sometimes refer to this layer of the massive biblical writ as "safe scripture."

Safety and justice are the issues in the several scriptural pronouncements concerning the so-called "Cities of Refuge." We hear a lot from the media about people mistakenly confined to long terms in prison when they were either innocent or wrongly accused. We shrug our shoulders, mutter something about how terrible it is, and then we change the channel.

Many years ago I visited a man who was serving a life term in a maximum-security facility for allegedly slaying a waitress with whom he had an argument. He was a Jewish fellow. Some of our Hebrew faithful still believe there are no incarcerated Jews, although that delusion may have been modified in light of the recent conviction of the man responsible for the worst investment scandal in history. This man is also Jewish.

An especially thoughtful archbishop serving the region—it was in the hilly southeastern corner of Ohio—had contacted me. "One of your folks has been asking to see a rabbi over at Lucasville Penitentiary. He doesn't want to talk to our Catholic chaplain anymore. Can you go down there? He seems to have something important to say, but he wants to say it to his own kind."

I made the time. I researched the convict's case. Charlie Cohen (not his real name) was convicted after the waitress and he struggled in an alley outside the diner where he often visited with her while ordering pancakes and coffee. No one saw them scuffle, but a gunshot drew a shocked, voyeuristic crowd. The revolver had been thrown or fell into a puddle of water. The woman's body was sprawled on the ground and she bled from her head into the same murky pool. Charlie was known to be irascible and unpredictable and he suffered frequent run-ins with the local police. Members of the gathering throng consistently reported that he was speechless and frozen as he stood over the victim. He submitted to police handcuffs and was escorted away and booked.

Although the weapon could not be successfully scrubbed for fingerprints or traced, Charlie was indicted, tried, and sentenced within a year of the incident. The county sheriff built a platform for himself atop this sensational case and was elected mayor of the community soon after. Charlie never confessed to the crime and said very little to anyone during the hurried proceedings. The local press labeled him with a disparagingly sensational moniker and converted the case into a media circus. The reticent Charlie was devoured by the mob culture that grew out of this event. He did look guilty. He did have some damning personal history. The jury sentenced him to life after less than three hours of deliberation.

As he was escorted out of the courthouse following the verdict, reporters encircled him. They yelled out to him: "What are you feeling, Charlie? Why did you do it? Don't you have anything to say?"

Charlie apparently spoke at last: "Just wish there had been someplace else to go. Some safe place." Reading that, my own curiosity about this man was heightened. The next day, I drove down to the heavily wooded, picturesque county of Scioto. I made my way onto the federal prison compound that sits ominously on a long, grizzled patch not that far from where the Ohio River winds into West Virginia.

I flinched as the heavy bars slammed behind me. Two tight-faced, well-armed guards accompanied me. We came to a final checkpoint. Another set of electric bars humming and banging. Then, the cellblock appeared and we entered a narrow visiting room. There was no window and no divider. Just a table and two chairs as I eyed Charlie, seated in a stained jump suit, with a series of numerals sown above his left shirt pocket. He looked like a gray weasel wearing thick, rimmed eyeglasses. He was painfully thin, with crooked, arthritic fingers that tapped nervously on the table. I felt an immediate meld of sympathy and disgust. The guards told me, politely, that they would be waiting just outside the open door.

"Sit down. I won't kill you." Charlie smiled, signifying that he was teasing me. I was offended by his very inappropriate opening.

"You asked for a rabbi and here I am. What would you like to say to me?"

"Sorry. Really, I am sorry."

"It's okay," I responded, genuinely. I noticed that his fingernails were long, yellowish, and neglected. It was not pleasant to be with him. Yet, it was, I had to admit, rather fascinating.

"I have a Chumash in my cell," he began. That is the Hebrew word for bound-edition of the Torah, or the Five Books of Moses. "They didn't let me bring it here for our visit. Maybe they were afraid I'd throw it at you." Now, Charlie giggled to himself and I felt a wave of nausea. I waited for him to speak some more. Then I noticed that his expression changed, from that of a defensive josher to that of a brokenhearted, lost soul. He looked up at me:

"Can you ask those guards out there for a Bible? They'll probably give it to you."

"Sure."

I stepped out and made the request. They agreed and I watched them retrieve a worn King James edition from a cabinet filled with various volumes and a supply of bottled grape juice and paper cups right there in the hallway. "A little vestry we got here, eh?" I said. The guards were not amused as one of them handed me the book.

Returning to Charlie, I saw that he was wiping tears from his face with a sleeve. It moved me to a softer attitude toward him. "Is there something in the Bible you'd like to discuss with me, Charlie?"

"Of course it's a Christian Bible they gave you?" A bit of the sneer returned.

"It's a Bible. It doesn't have a religion."

"Okay, I hear you. Would you sit with me and look up the Book of Daniel, chapter 12, verse 2?" I sat beside him, turned over the tattered pages of the book and located Daniel 12:2. The prisoner asked me to read it aloud:

And many of them that sleep in the dust of the earth shall awake, some to everlasting life, and some to shame and everlasting contempt.

"I'm really worried about her coming back to life." Charlie was shivering now.

"Who, Charlie?"

"Nancy."

"The woman you killed?"

"I did not kill her, Rabbi. I did not. I provoked her, yes. So I feel responsible. She called me out to the alley. She had my gun, from my apartment. It was my gun. I once pointed it at her. I'm a loser but I'm not a killer."

I looked back nervously; the guards were not visible. I asked Charlie to lower his voice, nonetheless. I said, "What do you mean, you didn't kill her? And why are you worried about her coming back to life? What are you telling me?"

"She came at me holding my pistol. She was real angry. I had called her terrible names so many times. We drank too much together. She stole money from my wallet all the time. She was crazed. I grabbed the gun from her and when I gripped it, it went off. God help me, it was an accident."

I believed Charlie.

"Why didn't you tell this to anybody?"

"Because it was my fault. The whole thing. I couldn't talk about it. Till now, today. And I was reading my Chumash and saw that in Daniel and I'm so afraid she will wake from the dead and get the shame and the everlasting condemnation. She don't deserve it." He put his head in his hands and began sobbing like a child. I stroked his thinning hair and rubbed his back, above the line on his penitentiary-issue shirt: CORRECTIONS.

He settled down after a few moments and looked to me for some kind of an answer, an aphorism, a sanction.

"Charlie," I said. "She's not coming back. She doesn't have to. You are already living 'the shame and the contempt' for her. You're sparing her that punishment. But why are you taking this jail sentence when the whole thing was an accident?"

He answered me immediately. "Because there was no place else for me to go. Nobody but me knew that it wasn't me, that I did not intend to kill her, and that she actually showed up with my pistol. Nobody would have ever believed me. They needed a murderer and they wanted a show. I had nowhere to go."

I left the downtrodden man and kept his revelations to myself. I was not in a position to discuss his statements with anyone. What I could not dismiss was his plaintive yearning for "somewhere to go"— under the circumstances. *How ironic*, I thought: *The old scripture, so co-opted by many clergy for guilt mongering, had a solution for the Charlies of the world three thousand years ago, for when our Hebrew ancestors took control of Canaan.* The blueprint is found in the Book of Deuteronomy:

> *Set apart three cities in the midst of the territory [God] has granted thee; cities that may be reached by well paved roads, and so placed as to divide up the whole of thy land into three districts. One of these must be near at hand, when blood has been shed and the slayer would take sanctuary. Such a man must be granted his life, on these conditions; the blow must have been struck unwittingly . . . to prevent the blood of innocent men being shed, here in this land the Lord is giving thee for thy own, and the guilt of that blood defiling thee.*

They were called "the Cities of Refuge," and we have nothing like them in the so-called "modern world." There would eventually be six such cities of sanctuary for men and women who had been set-up, wrongly convicted, or were simply innocent of the crimes for which they had been implicated or accused. Where is the shelter, the safety valve in this vulgar, self-righteous world in which both the ubiquitous media and the interminable terror have numbed us into platitudes or resignation when it comes to justice? Where does a person go when knowing that he or she is of innocent blood? They go crazy, that's where. That's what I think about when I think about Charlie, who eventually died alone, with his secrets, his agony, and his guiltiness, in that prison. And that is why I know the king must not have too many horses.

৩ ৎ৩

RABBI JOHANAN BEN ZAKKAI was as much a pragmatist as he was a sage. He understood about kings, horses, power, and how to spiritualize a religion with pastoral realism. Zakkai lived just a few decades after Christ when Judea was about to be entirely vanquished by the same Romans who had crucified Jesus. Zakkai was the one who originally proclaimed the axiom we considered at the beginning of this book: "If you are holding a sapling in your hand and someone tells you, 'Come quickly, the messiah is here!' First finish planting the tree and then go to greet the messiah."

In other words, known life at hand is more redemptive than an impulsive leap toward idealism. We have to know how to refute the spectacular (borrowing the phrase from the Indian novelist, Amit Chaudhuri) and faithfully manage the less exotic elements of day-to-day living. Religion fails us all too often because it demands that we build clouds in the sky when what we should do is erect hospitals on Earth, construct hunger centers, and—as we shall see in the case of Johanan ben Zakkai—build schools.

Johanan ben Zakkai literally saw the destruction of the city of Jerusalem on the part of the Romans coming. It was the year 70 CE and Rome had spent decades subjugating, torturing, enslaving, and murdering the Jewish residents of the beleaguered province, including the new Christian sect members among the Jews. The rabbi knew well there was no hope and the end of the Judean dominion was at hand and the people would no longer have access to the Temple Mount in order to offer their harvest sacrifices to God. The city was being choked, starved, and ravaged. There was no water to drink. Corpses rotted in the street, spreading disease and despair. Caesar's militias were running out of nails and wood to keep up with the systemic crucifixions that took place without stop, let alone any judicial process.

Zakkai devised an outlandish plan with a group of his disciples. He had them deceptively announce and spread the word that he had died. They placed him in a coffin and solemnly carried it beyond the city limits, ostensibly for burial. The "pallbearers" cautiously marched in the direction of the central Roman encampment, where the brigadier, Vespasian, an ambitious and ruthless candidate to become Caesar, was preparing the final assault.

Under cover, the disciples opened the casket and the determined rabbi stepped out. Alone, he marched straight into the Roman camp—much to the surprise and amusement of the startled legionnaires. Distracted by his moxie, the armored men did not run their swords through the straight-backed rabbi. In between chortles, they asked him: "And what can we do for you, Rabbi?"

"I should like to see your commander, Vespasian."

This was so bizarre that the warriors could not resist. "Of course, Rabbi. Immediately!"

Johanan ben Zakkai was escorted, with laughter and fascination, to Vespasian's lavish tent. Upon entering, he shrewdly announced: "Hail, Caesar!"

"Indeed?" The megalomaniac commandant enjoyed the greeting. He then listened carefully as the rabbi calmly prophesied that Vespasian and his legions would overrun and vanquish Jerusalem within days. He also declared that, as a result of Vespasian's stunning victory over the intractable Jews, the general would promptly succeed to the absolute leadership of the Roman Empire.

Suffice it to say that Vespasian was thoroughly pleased, charmed, and cajoled. He enjoyed the rabbi's spine-tingling savvy and begrudged the sage a layer of admiration:

"Well then, Rabbi, what can I give to you in return for your skills and courage?"

"Thank you, Caesar. If it pleases your highness, I simply ask your permission to gather my students who manage to survive your coming victory and allow us to open a school. We have a small academy in the town of Yavneh. All we ask is that you allow our remnant to peacefully study our Torah after you have completed your mission and become Emperor."

Vespasian pondered briefly. "Better you should study your damned scripture and not start up a new revolt against us after this battle is over. You have my permission and you are granted safe passage."

Johanan ben Zakkai, a paragon of spiritual pragmatism, did establish a Torah academy in Yavneh, which is a thriving small city in Israel today, a center of industry and aeronautics. The little school eventually expanded into the assembly place of the Sanhedrin, the supreme council of Jewish sages and clerics that produced laws and ideas for centuries.

Rome and its centurions are gone. When I walk along the Mediterranean coast near Yavneh, I pick up broken fragments of Roman pottery and dutifully deliver them to the Israel Antiquities office nearby. The waves dance in salty air and freedom. All the horses and chariots of Caesar could not defeat the power of an idea.

Chapter Thirteen

WHO'S TO SAY WHAT'S WRONG OR RIGHT?

"My religion is kindness."
—THE DALAI LAMA

I N HER 2012 BOOK, *Lots of Candles, Plenty of Cake*, the Pulitzer Prize-winning columnist and novelist Anna Quindlen ruminated about her Catholic upbringing as to why so much importance was given to "form" instead of focusing on devotion and "faith."

The same sentiments are carried around, like old sorrow, in the hearts of a vast segment of the seventy-six million baby boomers living in America today. One Pew research survey after another reports the precipitous decline of citizens who feel affiliated with any of the organized faith communities. The seminaries are painfully undersubscribed. Churches and synagogues are resorting to novel, sometimes desperate programming measures—from purely social gatherings, including "Rock Sabbaths" and "Christ Concerts," to creative, more accommodating scheduling of events to multimedia advertising to innovative daycare options to free dues for a year or more to in-house dating services to even the renovating of building spaces in favor of better light, contemporary seating, and Jumbotron LED screens.

To paraphrase a nationally known inspirational speaker, lamenting the churches' "descent toward irrelevance" and the coming specter of innumerable empty buildings: What could your church do to shift its schedule or abandon a one-size-fits-all Sunday morning service? Don't simply offer hymns and homilies on a Tuesday night, but rather reprogram your entire lineup. Ditch the large group-listening session and give attendees a chance to talk. Rely on small groups that are geographically convenient. Tie programming to social action.

In other words, don't just "do" church on Sunday mornings. "Be" church as often as possible so people have more chances to participate.

"*Be* church." That resonates with me and the noun can be any worship center of any denomination. "Be the change you want to see in the world," declared Mahatma Gandhi. And then the spiritual pragmatists come along, like Mother Teresa, with her admonition to us who are looking for a way, for a real path to fulfillment: "If you can't feed a hundred people, then feed just one." And from two thousand years ago, Rabbi Tarfon of the Talmud, said. "You are not required to complete the work but neither are you permitted to abstain from it."

Maybe the question is not so much, what can I believe? Maybe the question really is: What can I do? I once observed a group of Christians creating some real faith, some solid spirituality by applying their hands to the job rather than just using their mouths.

A Roman Catholic colleague had invited me to visit a children's hospital maintained by the local diocese in 1989. The lobby was streaked with color and scrubbed with hope. An air of comfort and cheerful urgency permeated the facility. However, the disciplined stillness was occasionally unsettled by careful whispers and furious cries. Science and faith, rationality and religiosity comingled everywhere, even as medical instruments glistened under sacramental icons that watched over the hallways and operating rooms.

Cancer-stricken kids—of all faiths—some of them bald, all of them brave, rested or played or teased one another in much light and under the attentive eyes of efficient and compassionate nurses. Many of these women, moving briskly in their ivory working shoes, were Sisters of Mercy. Their devotion to healing was and remains uncompromising— they appear to have no other purpose in life than to be God's agent of possibility.

Then my friend took me down a stairwell to the basement. "I want you to see something. And the whole point of it is that *nobody* sees it."

"Sees what?" I was curious and intrigued.

"We call it 'the blessing of the hands,'" the priest responded.

We made our way into a poorly lit laundry room. The pongs of detergent and bleach and the impress of steam were a stark contrast to the meticulous and precise design of the greater hospital building, with its chromatic reception areas, structured play areas, and glass elevators.

While several outsized washing machines hummed and adjacent dryers groaned, a small group of hushed workers were in motion around a rectangular table laden with a white, immaculate industrial-size tablecloth. The laborers, wearing rubber gloves, all of them Mexican immigrants steeped in church piety, were dipping a variety of gleaming surgical instruments in and out of steel bowls boiling in water and cleansers. They vigorously, almost rhythmically, wiped the sterilized instruments dry and laid them out in uniform rows across the table.

A moment or two after we two clerics arrived, a heavyset, aged nun, in wimple and veil, solemnly entered the area. Her eyes were vibrant as she approached the table. The workers stood at attention and all lifted their palms. The nun raised her wrinkled fingers a bit and spoke in a

Latin undertone to the assembled personnel. The simple dignity of the moment, the undeniable, sudden emotional sanctity that permeated, was palpable.

I realized the sister was blessing the hands of the workers. I grasped that, in anticipating the sanctification, the reverential staff was unable to have done anything less than absolutely and categorically disinfect the scalpels, scissors, forceps, dilators, and dissecting knives presented to them. I understood that the instruments would only then be antiseptically delivered to the physicians and nurses above.

It is stated in the rabbinic tradition that "The Bible hallows the lowliest acts—plowing, sowing, reaping, and the like—and elevates them into a service of God." The nobility of human labor is certainly rehearsed in scripture. "Working with your hands is the thing which is good" is stated in Ephesians. The writer of this book actually asserts here that people who keep a job will be less inclined to steal or depend on welfare.

James admonishes the upper classes: "Behold, the hire of the laborers who have reaped down your fields." So, when it comes to the old texts that the preachers are invoking, a lot of the material is about not preaching and not talking, but doing—building, laboring, endeavoring, creating, repairing, and planting.

Religion throws out more platitudes than we can handle and then distorts the spiritual landscape with a follow-up round of judgments. Read the Bible and you will actually discover a manual for labor, economic teamwork, and ethical behavior. Among Moses's final sermons encased in Deuteronomy, he tells corporate management to be fair and nondiscriminatory: "Don't take advantage," cries the retiring rabbi, "of a hired worker who is poor and needy." And he adds—just to head off any secondary bias—"whether that worker is a fellow Israelite or a foreigner living in your town."

Is there any question that the Bible, too often ripped off by moralizing men who want to control other people's wills, is steeped in the moral certitude of work? For the entire first week of Creation, all God did was labor. No prayers, no theologies, no sermons, just toil and formation. He designed, separated, spread out, inserted, implanted, watered, rearranged firmaments, and populated the fresh ground as well as the new seas. Scripture puts in plainly: "And for six days God worked, and on the seventh day he rested from his labors."

You can't argue with work and you can't knock a person down when he or she has created things that facilitate the needs of other people. Do you want to imitate God? Then create; don't pontificate. The hands of the workers are the tools of the angels. Read enough Bible and you find yourself studying the dignity of work. There's a lot more labor in the old writ than there is levitation.

And you will more likely be spared the exhausting grind of righteous debate. Like the dutiful hospital workers who clean surgical instruments and receive an impromptu nun's blessing, we are generally just trying to do the best we can. We then find some spiritual satisfaction in a quiet word of acknowledgment—more so than in a moment of staged high church. The same modest dynamic applies to the careworn teachers in our public schools, struggling to break through the din and violence of their urban adolescent pupils. These educators are rarely even begrudged a moment of benevolence and appreciation from the greater community, which increasingly evangelizes the political system, moralizes about teenage crime and pregnancy and indolence (often with racial insinuation) but doesn't even give these teachers and those kids a prayer at the ballot box.

More and more, the hard-working lower and middle classes are producing, manufacturing, and servicing while finding less and less that is inspiring in their houses of God. Exhausted, deprived of economic security, humiliated that their children are burdened with several times more debt than they ever were, they are disenchanted by rote liturgies and outsourced by hypocritical business codes that preach a new, mawkish religious patriotism and just break people's hearts.

A recent report from the Pew Research Center states there has been a decline in adult Christians in the US since 2007. Five million fewer adults in this country now identify with Christianity than did in 2007. Alarming drops in Jewish affiliation or even association have been described now for some three decades. Only the Muslim theological community is growing in numbers but the trend is worrisome for many, including purely observant Muslims, because the needle is turning toward, and melting into, the inferno of the jihadists.

The problem is that too few people are dictating for too many others what is right and what is wrong. This is a kind of moral tyranny that's not been seen since World War II. To my great sadness, I observe it in my own faith community, though it is hardly confined to the Jewish world. Regrettably, when I am in Jerusalem, I see and hear the maelstrom of judgmentalism and it is repugnant, particularly when approaching the plaza at the Western Wall. Men in religious garb, "theological police," spew invectives and bigotry at any and all who appear to be "un-Jewish" or "inappropriately dressed." Women are barred, and even pushed away, from equal prayer participation at the holiest Jewish shrine on Earth.

How different from my first visit there in July of 1967, just a few short weeks after Israel's "lightning victory" in the Six Day War. Responding to Jordanian artillery, Israeli forces entered the Old City and fought bitter hand-to-hand battles en route to recapturing and reuniting the divided city. The army then summarily drove out the Jordanian forces from the entirety of the "West Bank" of the Jordan River and ended the Hashemite Kingdom's own nineteen year occupation of this disputed territory.

I was fourteen years old, visiting from the United States, and walked through the Holy City with my older cousin, a twenty-two-year-old veteran of the June war. Every several hundred feet, small mounds of stones, still bloodstained, marked a place where a soldier had fallen. But the hot sun shone on a city golden with hope.

The Arab merchants in the grand market of winding alleys and endless shops welcomed us along with the fresh flood of business that came with the new rush of Israeli callers, as well as from manifold other lands. Peace and goodwill were in the air, along with the inviting smells of Turkish coffee, baking pita bread, sizzling meats, and countless exotic spices. The situation had not retrogressed into the contemporary Israeli-Palestinian crisis that subsequently devastated all aspirations for a harmonious Jerusalem and the peaceful coexistence of two states. Religious tribalism had not yet spoiled the harvest of possibilities that came with Israel's achievement that June.

My cousin and I alighted at the area of the Wall. There was no developed promenade yet, no re-laid stone walkways and modern arches, no rabbinic academies, and, most significantly, no formal barriers separating men from women. There was wonder and awe and a pervasive, nuanced mixture of reverence and grief. The Wall—the last retaining fragment of King Solomon's Holy Temple—loomed there with dusty, thickly weeded, raw splendor. No lines and no divisions were written or inscribed across that realm of sanctity. Nobody was telling anybody how to pray, how to weep, or how to thank.

Not so anymore; and this has nothing to do with the tragic confrontation between Jews and Muslims in the city. Go there as simply a Jew and you first have to get past the sense of being an intruder, even if you are incontrovertibly Jewish. This is because the landlords of the Wall, a government-sanctioned conglomerate of stern, bearded men from a variety of ecclesiastic tribes, are rather possessive of their default contract with the place. Unfortunately, especially for women, jurisdiction of the site is confined to the Orthodox rabbinate.

They scold you with their fierce eyes if you don't have a skullcap (though never examining your heart), and they imperiously ask you for money as if to pay for your unworthiness. They disdain the presence of sincere folks who are neither dressed for the seventeenth century nor given to the very disapproving tendencies that controvert the entire thesis of prayer.

I arrive with my own liturgy; I don't care what they think. But I do care that my mother, when she was living, and now her granddaughters are not permitted to pray in the same spaces as the oligarchic men who have co-opted the blood and yearning of Jewish history in favor of their sectarian plutocracy in Jerusalem.

My deal with the Wall is my own affair and it has evolved with the crises and upheavals and reversals and triumphs and breakthroughs of my life, and that is more honest than a chart of robotic prayers. Who are they to say what is a legitimate prayer or not and what is wrong and what is right? We have seen that the scripture, like fine leather, is flawed and inconsistent—what human yearning is carved in perfection?

When I touch the Wall, I feel godliness; no one can delineate what that is for you or me. I don't experience a simple-minded, gawking astonishment that is driven by guilty deference to the swaying rabbinical landlords who swarm about the place as thick as their black coats. I just don't believe God sees any difference between them in their traditional garb and me in my slacks and blazer. Neither they nor people like me— men or women—are exclusively correct or incorrect, just or unjust.

I place little notes in the wall but I don't think God has a minstrel on the other side of it that collects and annotates the pleas, names, and confessionals.

I follow the ritual because so many people have been doing this for so many centuries, and that the very cycle—with its uniformity and peacefulness and solemnity—instills the holiness that attends this place.

God is there, to paraphrase a more genuine rabbinical tradition, simply because we have let God in.

The millions of people—trembling, whispering, diverse, literate, uneducated and of many languages, journeys, dispositions, and wounds—who have been performing this custom of the private notes for so many centuries add up to the possibility of a divine spark in the open air of a city that both defines and defies peace.

On one occasion, I spoke to an old woman as I walked up the plaza from the Wall. Her eyes had seen more than mine ever will. The "religious police" had ejected her because she drifted too close to the men's section. She told me she had survived Treblinka and now had been pushed away from prayer in Jerusalem. Then she wished me a "Shabbat Shalom!" in Polish-inflected Hebrew.

Who could hear that and then require some passing rabbi to describe God for me? Better a saintly nun comes and simply blesses all the hands without distinguishing among the hands that do God's work. Better to remember that Abraham and Sarah's tent was open on four sides to welcome all who approach.

ON A TREK TO the Yucatan Peninsula and its environs not so long ago, something was reinforced for me that I had just learned during a Ramadan visit to the central mosque in San Diego, where I live. If we all just calmed down and listened to each other, we'd realize we're all drinking from the same well. We'd know that no good person is right and no other such person is wrong in the eyes of heaven; we're all doing the best we can and struggling with what the Catholics call *mysterium tremendum*—the great mystery of this life. When it comes to our predicament, our unyielding struggle with both eternity and mortality, religion may be the lyrics but spirituality is the song.

My family walked amidst the Chacchoben Mayan ruins a short distance from Costa Maya. It was muggy and exotic, and the horizon pressed against us. Our guide announced that we trekked along "the place where the sky begins." We were far from home but seemed close to the firmament.

Our well-spoken tour guide, an approachable man named Ivan, was fluent and enlightening. We listened carefully to his thoughtful ruminations about the wildlife and medicinal plants and the endless array of chipped relics, pottery, and clayed images. People and the earth and the gods and the inscrutabilities and the hopes and the rain and the calendar and the dreads were being described poetically in his spiritual vernacular. Yet it all sounded like a familiar dialect.

I realized again that we all have the same fears, dreams, anxieties, and enthrallments. Ivan, a thirtyish, articulate, ruggedly handsome man, was filled with ancestral mysticism and native blood. Remarkably—and to our great edification—he was actually born and raised on the very grounds that are now the carefully manicured national preserve of high-flung temples, archaeological sanctuaries, and moist rainforests.

Ivan explained to us about the coming Gregorian year of 2012—the subject of so much hyper-speculation, end-of-the-world prattle, and Western media exploitation. Indeed, 2012 did coincide with the end of a Mayan calendar cycle. But rather than being the "end of time" (a seemingly evangelical religious obsession), it was simply an exhilarating renewal of time, a resurgent numerical turnover, so much like the constantly renewable lunar cycles of the Torah and the Islamic almanacs. Standing in the shadow of one of the Mayan temples, I felt like I was at home in a celestial synagogue.

Moreover, the Mayan narrative of Creation is gratifyingly aligned with the Book of Genesis; the Mayans believe God first made humanity from sticks, then clay, and after two destructions, settled upon the fully realized Third Creation. All over this troubled world, there are peaceful, indelible moments when parents of all colors and creeds are telling the same stories to their children.

Thunder rolled incessantly, like the supervisory rumbles of ancient gods. We climbed the steps alongside the silent, looming pyramids and imagined the pieties and folklores of a proud civilization that still inspires awe and healing practices among the farmers, factory workers, medicine men, and tour guides of this old society. In the end, sun-god worshipers, polytheists, Mohammedens, Christians, Jews—we are all guided and lifted by our comparable stories.

Just a week earlier, I had visited (along with a small host of interfaith leaders) with the leader of San Diego's Islamic community to learn about, and then break that day's fast, during Ramadan. The Algerian-bred and scholarly young man who is the beloved imam here explained the holy month, its requirements and liturgies, and warmly invited us to share delicacies at the lunar conclusion of that day's observance and abstention.

The Imam explained that the full name of the month-long festival and introspection is "Ramadan Mubarak." Mubarak means "blessed." I couldn't help but mention in the dialogue that the word in Hebrew for "blessed" is remarkably similar, "*me-vu-rach.*" Nor did it escape my attention that we Jews, also a people of the lunar cycle, were about to embark upon our own fast of Yom Kippur. But then, when the Imam mentioned that the prophet Mohammed regularly fasted on Mondays and Thursdays, I was truly amazed: On Mondays and Thursdays, we Jews have always read from the Torah scroll and been particularly sensitive to the ebb and flow of holiness, time, and peaceful gestures.

On Mondays and Thursdays, Mohammed is fasting, Moses is studying, Jesus is blessing, and not a single measure of these things has anything to do with war, subjugation, or elitism. Not one of these devotional passages imposes the question of right or wrong; it's just all good.

There are moments when the religions can be selectively believed. But the moment any religion claims an absolute hold on belief, it ceases to be spiritually true. Maybe that is what so many people find troubling with the religion they grew up with—today they are unsure of what to believe. As children grow up and study science and physics and literature, many often begin to question the faith they learned from their parents. We may all find encouragement in what an anonymous Native American once declared: "If you take a copy of the Bible and put it out in the wind and the rain, soon the paper on which the words are printed will disintegrate and the words will be gone. Our Bible *is* the wind."

Good God, why are we fighting, when we all are so tenderly linked in the reassuring rhythm of old stories? Who's to say what's right or wrong?

Chapter Fourteen

THE TEN COMMANDMENTS ARE ALL YOU NEED

❦

"All the other commandments are subsumed in the Ten Commandments."
—Rabbi Shlomo Yitzchaki (Rashi)

W HEN I REACHED THE crest of Mount Sinai in 1979 and there performed the Bat Mitzvah ceremonies of two exhilarated American girls, I saw the sun rise over a terrestrial glory that resonated with both spiritual and physical transcendence. As paint-like streaks of morning light broke through, we beheld the jagged landscape of adjacent, reddish, biblical mountains and a horizon that hung like the gateway to heaven. We gazed at the purple riverbeds below, the distant coral reefs, and the *wadi* formations. Ospreys flew by, nodding at our awareness of clear, natural holiness. There was history in the hills, borne aloft on spiritual wings.

Our group of sixty youngsters, we three guides, and an armed Israeli soldier had started climbing at 3:00 A.M. We ascended the mountain in a circular fashion, following the traditional steps of Moses who is said to have made the journey, alone, in approximately 1358 BCE.

We were hiking up to the summit where millions of people have believed for thousands of years that Moses met God and received two tablets of stone. While Moses shielded his eyes from the celestial heat and light, God inscribed the Ten Commandments with his own fingertips. So arriving there, I was moved and lifted: The legend has earned its own truth because so many good people have sworn its integrity. And the integrity, with its attendant rapture, comes from the hard legacy of the tale; somehow, some way, we have been left with the basic natural laws of human life.

It doesn't matter if Moses actually climbed up that mountain or not. What matters is that we as a human family have come down from it with what Moses (whoever he was) was trying to teach us. And how he educated us about acting like human beings is all we need to know to live together in peace.

So when I blessed those two young women at the crest that morning, in that sky-borne sanctuary that all the faiths believe in, I did feel the presence of God and an inspiring layer of sacred history.

Sadly, ever since Sinai, the religions have bled one another dry over one controversy after another. We have killed one another over the question of Jesus, what a miracle is or isn't, over the provenance of the city of Jerusalem, about which is the "true church," who is a "Torah-Jew," and whether Sunnis or Shiites are the verifiable messengers of Mohammed. We have succumbed to spiritual insecurity and to the pitiful need so many people have to make themselves feel bigger by making other people smaller.

And yet, all the faiths find common ground in the Ten Commandments. Maybe this is because the commandments are not religious dictates as much as they are a simple, straightforward declaration of ethics. Don't steal. Don't covet someone else's spouse. Don't malign your neighbor. Don't worship idols. Don't murder a person.

It is a tribute to the pragmatic honesty of the scriptural literature that almost every character referenced in the stories, both before and after the revelation of the commandments in the Book of Exodus, freely breaks one or more the laws. Just like we all do. Cain murders his brother; Sarah banishes the child Ishmael to the desert; Rebekah dishonors parental discretion by appropriating a birthright; Moses kills an Egyptian; Miriam blasphemes God's racial values; David commits serial adultery. None of the offenders breach the Commandments because they are Jews or Midianites or Egyptians, priests or prophets or pagans. They break them because they are people—human and flawed.

Still, the Ten Commandments are all one needs when it comes to divinity and belief because they cover all scenarios, they apprehend all human flaws and yearnings, and they include everybody. They don't divide people; they distinguish between behaviors. And the root of this accomplishment is discovered in the opening phrase of this eternal memo: "I am the Lord your God." One God for all humans. "Your God . . ." —not this one's or that one's. No ethnic group or creed is invoked; it's a moment of heavenly generics. One set of morals for all folks living on the only planet known to contain human life.

And these laws were not declared in anybody's church or at a particular faith convention. They were not proclaimed in Rome, Jerusalem, or in Mecca. They came down from a mountain in the middle of a desert—just as life and its problems and its threats and its temptations come at us out of the wilderness of our unpredictable and capricious existences.

Rabbi Menachem Schneersohn was the famed "Lubavitcher Rebbe" certain fundamentalist Jews affirm will return to Earth as the Messiah. "The Rebbe," who ran a theological autocracy out of Brooklyn, New York, wrote a missive about the Ten Commandments in 1964, stating that the commandments begin with "I am," which is a tenet of monotheism.

Schneersohn was picking up on the opening words of the Decalogue: "I am the Lord your God, who brought you out of Egypt." *Wait a minute*, he was likely thinking. The first commandment is declarative, not a

"Do-Not." It means, "Worship only one deity and that would be me." So the ten laws begin with harmony and a unifying source. The heavily browed sage shook with excitement and piety. Like many deep-feeling mystics, he was following an old folklore: Each one of us is supposed to imagine that we were physically present at the Sinai revelation and also received these simple rules of civilization.

Here's the bottom line: The sun isn't God; the Nile River isn't God; Pharaoh certainly is not God. Like so much of the Hebrew scripture, the ideas and the actions are a response to Egypt. Ancient Egypt, though filled with art and science and folklore, was still a harsh place. It was about slavery and subjugation and degradation, and it was a culture that replaced a heavenly, unseen God with divine interlopers—deific statues, rivers, snakes, pyramid tombs, and powerful men and their magicians who had no concept of human dignity.

So one reason the Ten Commandments are all you need is because they rescue religious values back from enchantments and clichés to a basic, rational concept: Slavery is wrong; freedom is right. The God that is self-quoted on the chiseled stones and across history is first and foremost about liberty. This is the God I pray to—the God that props up our culture rather than smashing it into sectarian combat zones.

This God on the mountain that Moses went up to see doesn't promote himself as the God of creation or the God that designed Sabbath or even the God of any specific people. This is the God that a strongly secular Abraham Lincoln venerated when he recognized African slaves were human beings. In 1858, more than two years before his momentous presidency, Lincoln boomed in a debate: "Our reliance is in the love of liberty which God has planted in our bosoms."

This is the God that Sojourner Truth—the first black woman to win a lawsuit in the United States (she obtained her son's freedom from slave-owners)—a former bondswoman herself and then a fiery abolitionist, preached about across the nation. (Born Isabella Truth in 1827, the future Sojourner was sold into slavery in New York State at the age of ten for the sum of $100.00 and a few sheep.) This is the God that Anne Frank inscribed in her diary. This is the God that Dr. Martin Luther King, Jr. entreated when he stated, with his hallmark intuition about this life and its heartbreaks.

So the Bible is working for me in the Ten Commandments because it's not offering me bromides about good and evil or trying to frighten me into submission with theatrical miracle-dramas. It's telling me that the first thing I should be doing as a human being is helping others to be free. It is educating me that slavery—from Egypt to ISIS—is ruthlessly wrong and sinful. It's not informing me how to be kosher. It's telling me how to be human. I've studied a number of scholarly statements from the evangelical and even the Puritan communities that affirm the spiritual transcendence of the Ten Commandments over all other scriptural laws and declarations.

Here is the text of the commandments, according to the "Revised Standard Version" from 1952. This version is generally agreed to by Jewish and Christian sources. The words are found in chapter 20 of the Book of Exodus, and then reiterated, in slightly different versions, in both Leviticus and Deuteronomy.

1. I am the Lord your God, who brought you out of the land of Egypt, out of the house of bondage.
2. You shall have no other gods before me.
3. You shall not make for yourself a graven image, or any likeness of anything that is in heaven above, or that is in the earth beneath, or that is in the water under the earth;

you shall not bow down to them or serve them; for I the Lord your God am a jealous God, visiting the iniquity of the fathers upon the children to the third and fourth generation of those who hate me, but showing steadfast love to thousands of those who love me and keep my commandments.

4. You shall not take the name of the Lord your God in vain; for the Lord will not hold him guiltless who takes his name in vain.

5. Remember the Sabbath day, to keep it holy. Six days you shall labor, and do all your work; but the seventh day is a Sabbath to the Lord your God; in it you shall not do any work, you, or your son, or your daughter, your manservant, or your maidservant, or your cattle, or the sojourner who is within your gates; for in six days the LORD made heaven and earth, the sea, and all that is in them, and rested the seventh day; therefore the Lord blessed the Sabbath day and hallowed it.

6. Honor your father and your mother, that your days may be long in the land which the Lord your God gives you.

7. You shall not kill.

8. You shall not commit adultery.

9. You shall not steal.

10. You shall not bear false witness against your neighbor.

11. You shall not covet your neighbor's house; you shall not covet your neighbor's wife, or his manservant, or his maidservant, or his ox, or his ass, or anything that is your neighbor's.

Before etching anything in stone, incidentally, we must note: There isn't a consensus that the Ten Commandments amount to ten! Some critics find sixteen regulations imprinted; I personally see thirteen. The dissertation about this extends beyond the churches and synagogues and it's another favorable aspect of scripture—that it can and should spark debate. Religion without debate is a frozen river. Religion with some spirit is the same river, only now it is moving water.

The First Amendment Center at Vanderbilt University, which analyzes legal issues, states: "Religious groups ... vary in how they divide the text into ten." So much for absolute religious arithmetic, though these ten or more commandments add up to a concise civilized summation that does more good on paper than a thousand windy homilies.

As mentioned, I can extrapolate thirteen commandments on the ancient tablets. For example, the first two lines ("I am the Lord your God" and then "You shall have no other gods but me") are really two separate matters. The traditional third commandment, about the Sabbath, may also be viewed as comprising two: The first is to celebrate a Sabbath, to actually lay down your burdens and rest as against the unforgiving stress of work and turmoil that consume us all week long. To create a buffer against the madness, the invasiveness, and the viciousness that pounds against our ears day after day.

The second law within this double statute simply prohibits toiling on that day—establishing the basis for fair labor laws and respect between staff and management. There just has to be a twenty-four-hour interval in the week when the clock is not the tyrant, when the boss is not in charge. It's not even about which day it is; it's about that there *is* such a day. The religions hardly concur on when the Sabbath is; the Muslims designate Friday; the Jews, Saturday; and the Christians, Sunday. The soul needs the reprieve of the day and doesn't really obsess with the calendar timing.

But no matter, the universal understanding is that there are Ten Commandments and even the Bible favors neat packages. The cachet here is simplicity. And the Decalogue is a tenfold compendium of goodwill and ethics that starts with a freedom-loving God, bypasses all partisan influences, and makes a comprehensive psychic covenant with humanity. The keyword is "you."

You should not build idols. *You* should not kill. *You* should not steal, have sex with somebody else's spouse, or steal somebody else's property. And by implication, *you* should observe a Sabbath—meaning that you will benefit from the relief and refreshment that are an antidote to the tension, the traffic, the nonstop (and disheartening) news broadcasts, and the fixation with all those cyber devices that are constantly bombarding your head with astonishingly superfluous and distracting data.

The Sabbath, which is chartered in these rock-bottom laws, may be about church prayer for some—which is often curative and redemptive. It is good to create a community of kindred hopes. But the Sabbath is really about an ancient spiritual innovation: Setting aside a restorative day so that you are again present in the lives of people you love and who love you. The Sabbath is the opposite of Facebook. It's a weekly bridge from the chaos to the calmness. It's a regular sabbatical that gets you back in sync with the world around your heart after the world has whirled around your head for six pounding days.

It's about looking into the faces of your children rather than passing them quickly, with the perfunctory "Everything good?" on your hurried way out the door. Talking with people as opposed to texting them. Discovering their fears and joys and wounds and successes. Using your imagination instead of recycling information. Cherishing memory as the collaboration of your soul and intellect rather than the calibration of available megabytes. Gaining knowledge and insight from unhurried and fascinating conversations. Breathing, singing, playing, lingering. And, by Talmudic dictate, making love! Yes, the pragmatic rabbinic literature knows that it is good for you to enjoy sexual intimacy with your beloved on the day you are not distracted by anything but your feelings for and your history with that person.

The Ten Commandments are lean, accessible, and intuitive about human life. In this twenty-first century of extreme religious bedlam and cluttered digital dependence, they are our best bet for cleansing the soul and calming the heart.

We are so tired! The world we live in is grueling and threatening and it slams our psyches with social unrest, economic uncertainty, and fluctuating hopes. We drift off in our thoughts and recall "the old days"— there were just three to five TV channels, a local newspaper that you read leisurely and in your hands, a set of rules that made us feel protected and, yes, there was something called childhood. A long-distance phone call brought with it the heady impression of technological marvel and, well, distance. It was a big deal.

We didn't already know everything by the time we were seven years old, and there was a delicious sense of mystery that led us all along the path to adulthood.

That gnawing dread that follows us around now, that the world is nuts, that people are crazy, that iconic buildings are vulnerable, that nothing works, that our country is not what it used to be—this stuff we think and worry about is simply not being serviced by the old tribal regulations and habits that twist the religious texts and lack the moral clarity of the Ten Commandments.

We pine for a shield against the unrelenting spiral of events—the bizarre new medical epidemics, from Ebola to Avian Influenza A; the typhoons, earthquakes, and droughts; the unfathomable, omnipresent terrorism; the anthrax scares; the political shakiness and electoral venality; and, yes, the blatant immorality that seeps through organized religion. We are weary of the shenanigans of church leaders who camouflage each other's depravities, who deny women respect. All the while, these religious feudalists are telling us what truth is, what civilized behavior is, even though it's been there in the old scripture for over three thousand years—in the Ten Commandments.

The thing to remember is that the entire document, consisting of just 313 words, is written in spiritually generic language. The words "Jew" or "Christian" appear nowhere. No nationality is mentioned but for the reference to Egypt as the place from which "you" were freed. Israel, Christianity, messianic promises, priests, doctrine, tribes—none of these words or concepts are found anywhere in the most universally embraced set of basic principles ever presented to this world.

It was all addressed to "you." It was not addressed to angels. It was not dispatched to a selective mailing list of church councils. You are preapproved for participation just by virtue of being a child born to God.

With verbal economy, it covers every dimension of human decorum and conduct. It gives you an uncontested God, a bottom-line value (freedom), and a family heritage. The latter derives from the fourth commandment, which not only tells you to "honor your father and mother," but also serves as a paragon of spiritual pragmatism.

Notice the admonition is not to "love" your father and mother. That does not mean you cannot or should not love your parents, whether in this life or in memory. But it does leave open the reality, widely experienced in this life, that not every man or woman who ever created or adopted children were successful parents, worthy of adoration. Rather than kowtowing to theological idealism, this is a matter of spiritual common sense, another way to make peace with your religion.

In my own case, loving my departed parents, both of whom were afflicted with psychological deficiencies and emotional disabilities, has been a challenge. When I read the Bible, I relate to the many examples of family dysfunction that we have already alluded to in this book. Like Jacob, my parents played favorites among their children—the burden of this has now strained a third generation. Like King Saul, my father was a brilliant misanthrope stricken with violent tendencies. As Rebekah was a schemer, my mother manipulated legacies and deceived my father; my brother and I have never really found the peace as a result.

I remember our kitchen table was not often a peaceable place. There were simmering resentments and latent volatility and a disturbing sense that someone would snap or condemn or threaten at any time. Melodramatic, screaming exits from the meal were too often endured and remain the stuff of nightmares decades later.

So I'm left with the burden of how to deal with the emotional yoke of my mother and father. In an exceptional burst of spiritual pragmatism, scripture gives me a safety valve of decency and realism. I don't have to love them. I do have to honor them. And where did I learn this? Not in any running, fear-mongering, sectarian portion of scripture that would only add to the sense of despairing divisiveness already infecting my life. No, I found it in the theological neutrality of the Ten Commandments. I found it in a supreme set of ideas that didn't pull me apart from anybody else.

I don't have to patronize my family story with anecdotes I don't feel or practice rituals I don't embrace. Yet I can make peace with the story by simply honoring its existence in the fabric of my life. And this is when scripture is working for me and not against me.

There is another element to the Ten Commandments story that reveals scripture's ability to discern human life in a rational matter. It has to do with the curious timing of the event at Sinai, when Moses purportedly received the two tablets of the law.

The Bible is clear: Sinai and the giving of the Commandments, happened seven weeks after the Hebrews departed Egypt. In fact, there is a major Jewish festival called Shavuot (which means weeks) that is celebrated precisely forty-nine days after Passover (the anniversary of the march out of Egypt). Shavuot commemorates the giving of the Ten Commandments.

So the question is: Why did God wait all those weeks before revealing the Law? Why stall? Why not pull back the curtain immediately as part of the opening of the freedom march?

Here is where scripture is again working for me. It is recognizing that people, from infants transitioning from crawling to walking and adults adjusting to sudden changes in their lives, need time to absorb the new terrain and acclimatize to shifting circumstances. The Hebrew slaves, cowering in dread and doubt as they bolted from Pharaoh, and then immediately taking in the cosmic works of God (devastating plagues, parting seas, and thundering mountains) were likely more afraid of their new deity, this "Yahweh," than of the Egyptian gods they had just fled.

The problem with religious miracles is that they thrash manageable perceptions and are ultimately heavenly placebos for earthly situations. The solutions offered by spiritual pragmatism are grounded in their patience for human fears, flaws, and faults. Those fugitives in the desert, referred to by scholar Thomas Cahill as "the dusty ones," didn't even know this Moses. How could they be expected to instantly become infatuated with this new God called Yahweh?

People who have been enslaved all their lives, who are illiterate, who've been ingrained to view themselves as less than human, cannot be expected to suddenly grasp the meaning of liberty and law and the notions of civilized behavior and fair play. Scripture is cogent and intuitive here: after a reasonable period of transition, they'd be better equipped to consider and grasp new ideas and mind-boggling concepts about life and about themselves. It takes a little bit of time to pass from degradation to dignity.

We saw this process fail catastrophically in the United States following the supposed liberation of the slaves in the South: The Emancipation Proclamation signed by President Lincoln on January 1, 1863, turned out to be just that—a proclamation. The enchained Africans were technically free inasmuch as they were still living in Confederate states that tenaciously remained outside the jurisdiction of the federal government.

The Ten Commandments, which profess no color or racial or cultural or gender preferences, are scripture's finest testament to the value of spiritual equanimity. And they were delivered (according to the narrative and its attendant moral message) within a normal interval and after the Hebrews could adapt to their new landscape of opportunity and responsibility.

You cannot assume people will effortlessly morph from bondage to self-esteem. It requires a period of reflection and thinking. Religious and social tyranny will never work because they rob people of the ability to think.

Religion tells you what to think; spirituality tells you, simply, *to think*.

So in this sensible story, God delayed seven weeks before invoking the commandments. Bringing them down on confused and frightened heads the day after they departed Egypt might have been very dramatic. It certainly would have been dizzying and debilitating. Spare us the drama, oh theologians, and let us reflect on the ideas! Give us the time to become believers, not just followers.

PEOPLE SOMETIMES ASK ME, which of the Ten Commandments is the most important? In talking about it, many folks opine that it's the first one, "I am the Lord your God," because inaugurating a benevolent creator, a safe source for our prayers, seems paramount. Others argue that the most imperative law is "You shall not kill." It is always interesting to ponder and it invites a moment of free spiritual and ethical discourse. When we exchange ideas, theological harshness is leavened by pastoral kindness.

Meanwhile, I think the traditional number four, "Honor your father and mother," offers the most philosophical merit for the human family. It's the one I choose because it harvests all the others.

Again, it is logical; it does not compel love when love is hard to express or feel. But it does oblige reverence for your birth or adopted family. And when you revere where you came from (as you undeniably came from your parents, no matter their blemishes), then you respect yourself and you know who you are.

When you are in touch with your lineage, you value yourself, and are more likely to value others. You will treasure life more than a wandering soul who has no place to alight. You will less likely kill, you perhaps won't steal, you maybe won't lie about your neighbors, and you won't necessarily covet their loved ones and their possessions. You will have a category of inner peace that unhappy people crave and that too often drives them to unacceptable or even criminal behavior. When you know who you are, you are simply less liable to take anything from someone else. When you know your name and are comfortable with it, it can even save your life.

A story is told from the darkest days: A rabbi lived in the Polish village of Danzig as the storm clouds began to bring in the Nazis in the late 1930s. The war and the slaughter were coming; even those who pretended it all wasn't impending knew in their hearts that terrible things were brewing.

It was the rabbi's custom to take a daily morning walk in the village and to greet every person he met. In spite of everything, the rabbi was determined to emit cheerful good spirits. At the outskirts of the town, he would hail a rather unfriendly Polish *Volksdeutche* (an ethnic German) named Muller.

"*Gutmorgen*, Herr Muller," the rabbi would declare.

"*Gutmorgen*, Herr Rabbiner," came the reply.

This happened every day, until the warfare and the genocide of the Jews devoured Europe. Herr Muller donned an SS uniform and the rabbi, like almost every single Polish Jew, would be engulfed by the night. The fact is that the rabbi lost every member of his family in the death camp of Treblinka, and eventually wound up being deported to Auschwitz.

Now the rabbi was herded off the ghastly cattle train and, wearing a grimy striped uniform, his head and beard shaven and his eyes sick with starvation and disease, he stood in the selection line. It was morning but no one was greeting anyone else during a restorative walk.

An ominously severe man wearing white gloves and a crisp military uniform sat at a desk and pointed each Jew in a direction: "Right! Left, left, left!" Right was life, left was immediate death. The rabbi drew near the table, and saw the SS officer who did not look up momentarily. The rabbi hardly believed what he realized.

Gathering all his remaining strength and courage, the rabbi said: "*Gutmorgen*, Herr Muller."

The officer slowly looked up. A faint smile of recognition was visible under the dark cap adorned with skull and bones. "*Gutmorgen*, Herr Rabbiner." The hand went up and pointed—right.

The rabbi did not start reciting Psalms. He did not make a plea based on Christian mercies. He did not ask for anything "in the name of God." He simply called out to his enemy by name. And so the rabbi lived to tell the story.

This is a most exceptional case, obviously. But it tells us that when a human face and a human voice intervene in the relentless cavalcade of hate, then we will more likely live together. And a life was saved because two men in hell suddenly recalled their homes, their mothers and fathers, their own fleeting associations, and the many times they had acknowledged their identities. The rabbi insured all this by assertively stamping the humanity of both men during so many morning walks back in Danzig and before the world went mad.

We will all never share the same theologies, and we will never overcome our dangerous insecurities—our need to conquer and subdue. But we will always share our humanity, particularly when we choose spiritual pragmatism over religious division.

I know the Bible has some hateful passages, such as those that denounce homosexual love and demand stoning for less-than-felonious crimes. But I prefer to think about the Bible that tells me "not to put a stumbling block before the blind" and not "to stand by idly while your neighbor bleeds." I choose the Bible that tells me freedom trumps everything and that endorses Moses's love for an African woman.

I know the Bible contains military orders for the Hebrews to unmercifully wipe out the residents of Canaan and then settle on their land. I prefer to think about the Bible that instructs soldiers to go around an orchard when on their march to battle and that admonishes farmers to let the soil rest and refresh itself every seventh year.

I know the Bible sometimes makes deplorable distinctions between races and peoples. But I prefer to think about the Bible that expects Hebrew soldiers who have captured a female prisoner of war to immediately grant her privacy, allow her to comb her hair, and trim her fingernails because she is a person and not an object for their consumption. And she is pardoned and allowed to return to her home.

And I know a huge section of Leviticus, which is otherwise filled with grotesque directives about lepers, dead bodies, and blood sacraments, is nonetheless the literary home of the first and most magnanimous system of incremental slave-liberation in history. Every seven years, coinciding with the sabbatical of the land, some bondsmen are released. It's clocked into the calendar. Then, in the Jubilee Year (the fiftieth), everybody goes free. The famous biblical proclamation is inscribed on the Liberty Bell encased in Philadelphia's Independence Park:

> *Proclaim liberty throughout the land unto all the inhabitants thereof*

I know my tradition asserts, "The Torah was not given to angels." Perfection is neither demanded from nor expected of its characters or its readers. We are not impeccable and most of us are doing the best we can. To paraphrase Lincoln: The Scripture, through all its twists and turns, and with the fingerprints of its numerous authors, is ultimately "by, for, and of the people." As the sagacious Hillel wrote in the Talmud, "In a place where there are no human beings, you strive to be a human being." No wonder Jesus emulated Hillel and revisited the scholar's lessons almost one hundred years later when he taught others in the Galilee.

I DID NOT WRITE this book to argue with the churches and the synagogues. My concern is not about the buildings. It's about what is too often being transmitted in those places and by whom. I am a professional veteran of the synagogue culture and am hardly interested in simply disparaging a community that has done much good for hundreds of centuries. But I also believe (and the more principled texts in the library of scripture affirm) that we are all simply the children of God.

In the case of my own people: We Jews parented Christianity and Islam. So who more than us should be reaching out to the other faith families? In the matter of my profession: The world has grown choleric from religious disharmony and intransigence. Young people, from Europe to the Middle East, from the Pacific to the Indian Oceans, are jaded and disillusioned with the misappropriating of spirituality by the tyrants of faith. They want to be unrestricted to discover the God who started this planet by planting a garden in Eden and then setting people loose from the bondage of Pharaohs.

In America, the demographics have shifted beyond any point of return. We are intermarrying at historic rates and we are (when not corrupted by religious despots) accepting one another, learning about each other's customs, rituals, songs, and foods in a manner that can only please the heaven that all religions claim is our reward. So then, we clergy should become part of the solution, not part of the problem.

Where is the truth? Just as I am skeptical of the indulgent dramas that comprise so much of scripture, that's how much I avow its intermittent psychological brilliance. Where is the instruction, after all? The answer, the solution, is found, revealingly, in Deuteronomy:

> *For this instruction, which I instruct you this day, is not concealed from you, nor is it far away. It is not in heaven, that you should say, "Who will go up to heaven for us and fetch it for us, to tell it to us, so that we can fulfill it?" Nor is it beyond the sea, that you should say,*

*"Who will cross to the other side of the sea for us and fetch it for us,
to tell it to us, so that we can fulfill it?" Rather, this thing is very close
to you; it is in your mouth and in your heart, so that you can fulfill it.*

Yes, this is when the old Bible is working for me, and this is when
I can make some sense out of the dictates of faith: "This thing is very
close to you; it is in your mouth and in your heart . . ."

I have a brain, I have a heart, and I have a stake in this universe! I was
not born to subsist as a robot. I do not require any ordinances from any
assemblage beyond those that move me to repair the world. Otherwise I
am calcified, not inspired.

And as for the religious buildings mentioned just above, I find
their absolution in the Book of Exodus, the same book that gives us the
world's first civil rights movement: There we read: "Let them build me
a sanctuary, so that I may dwell among them."

Notice: We are not instructed to construct churches and synagogues
for some kind of homeless God. "To dwell among *them*." So it turns out
that God doesn't live inside buildings. God lives inside you. When you
know and accept that, then that's when you make spiritual peace not just
with your religion, but also with yourself.

ACKNOWLEDGMENTS

I AM GRATEFUL FOR the efforts of my literary agent, Jill Kramer, who was tireless in finding a publishing home for this work. Then it became a professional and creative joy to work with Nancy Schenck, executive editor of Central Recovery Press. Nancy embraced this book and mentored me in its completion with great enthusiasm and high standards.

Many thanks to Eugene Schwartz, author, editor, and publisher—and my dear friend. Gene arranged for me to meet Bill Gladstone, head of Waterside Productions, who then graciously accepted me into his venerable agency. Gene has taught me the meaning of dignity and of earned wisdom, and he has my deepest respect and gratitude.

Every moment of the day of every day, all over this troubled world, human beings are wrestling with the concept of God and their longing for a tender godliness to develop among us. To them—the anonymous dreamers of the human spirit, the true believers in the kindness of angels—I am most obliged for the inspiration of this book.

Also Available from Central Recovery Press

BEHAVIORAL HEALTH

Irrelationship: How We Use Dysfunctional Relationships to Hide from Intimacy
Mark Borg, Jr., PhD; Grant Brenner, MD; Daniel Berry, RN, MHA · $16.95 US
ISBN: 978-1-942094-00-5 · E-book: 978-1-942094-01-2

Wisdom from the Couch: Knowing and Growing Yourself from the Inside Out
Jennifer L. Kunst, PhD · $16.95 US · ISBN: 978-1-937612-61-0
E-book: 978-1-937612-62-7

*Hard to Love: Understanding and Overcoming
Male Borderline Personality Disorder*
Joseph Nowinski, PhD · $15.95 US · ISBN: 978-1-937612-57-3
E-book: 978-1-937612-58-0

Many Faces, One Voice: Secrets from The Anonymous People
Bud Mikhitarian · $17.95 US · ISBN: 978-1-937612-93-1
E-book: 978-1-937612-94-8

A Man's Way through Relationships: Learning to Love and Be Loved
Dan Griffin, MA · $15.95 US · ISBN: 978-1-937612-66-5
E-book: 978-1-937612-67-2

Love in the Land of Dementia: Finding Hope in the Caregiver's Journey
Deborah Shouse · $15.95 US · ISBN: 978-1-937612-49-8
E-book: 978-1-937612-50-4

*Dancing in the Dark: How to Take Care of Yourself
When Someone You Love Is Depressed*
Bernadette Stankard and Amy Viets · $15.95 US · ISBN: 978-1-936290-70-3
E-book: 978-1-936290-83-3

Disentangle: When You've Lost Your Self in Someone Else
Nancy L. Johnston, MS, LPC, LSATP · $15.95 US · ISBN: 978-1-936290-03-1
E-book: 978-1-936290-49-9

Game Plan: A Man's Guide to Achieving Emotional Fitness
Alan P Lyme; David J Powell, PhD; Stephen R Andrew, LCSW · $15.95 US
ISBN: 978-1-936290-96-3 · E-book: 978-1-937612-04-7

The Light Side of the Moon: Reclaiming Your Lost Potential
Ditta M Oliker, PhD · $16.95 US · ISBN: 978-1-936290-95-6
E-book: 978-1-937612-03-0

MEMOIRS

Bottled: A Mom's Guide to Early Recovery
Dana Bowman · $16.95 US · ISBN: 978-1-937612-97-9
E-book: 978-1-937612-98-6

Body Punishment: OCD, Addiction, and Finding the Courage to Heal
Maggie Lamond Simone · $15.95 US · ISBN: 978-1-937612-81-8
E-book: 978-1-937612-82-5

Weightless: My Life as a Fat Man and How I Escaped
Gregg McBride · $17.95 US · ISBN: 978-1-937612-69-6
E-book: 978-1-937612-70-2

Acrobaddict
Joe Putignano · $17.95 US · ISBN: 978-1-937612-51-1
E-book: 978-1-937612-52-8

Rage: The Legend of "Baseball Bill" Denehy
Bill Denehy with Peter Golenbock · $16.95 US · ISBN: 978-1-937612-55-9
E-book: 978-1-937612-56-6

From Harvard to Hell . . . and Back:
A Doctor's Journey through Addiction to Recovery
Sylvester "Skip" Sviokla III, MD with Kerry Zukus · $16.95 US
ISBN: 978-937612-29-0 · E-book: 978-1-937612-30-6

Dark Wine Water: My Husband of a Thousand Joys and Sorrows
Fran Simone, PhD · $15.95 US · ISBN: 978-1-937612-64-1
E-book: 978-1-937612-65-8

Finding a Purpose in the Pain:
A Doctor's Approach to Addiction Recovery and Healing
James L Finley, Jr., MD · $15.95 US · ISBN: 978-1-936290-71-0
E-book: 978-1-936290-84-0

The Mindful Addict: A Memoir of the Awakening of a Spirit
Tom Catton · $18.95 US · ISBN: 978-0-9818482-7-3 · E-book: 978-1-936290-44-4

Some Assembly Required: A Balanced Approach
to Recovery from Addiction and Chronic Pain
Dan Mager, MSW · $16.95 US · ISBN: 978-1-937612-25-2
E-book: 978-1-937612-26-9

RELATIONSHIPS AND RECOVERY

All Bets Are Off: Losers, Liars, and Recovery from Gambling Addiction
Arnie and Shelia Wexler with Steve Jacobson · $16.95 US
ISBN: 978-1-937612-75-7 · E-book: 978-1-937612-76-4

Making Peace with Your Plate: Eating Disorder Recovery
Robyn Cruze and Espra Andrus, LCSW · $16.95 US · ISBN: 978-1-937612-45-0
E-book: 978-1-937612-46-7

Loving Our Addicted Daughters Back to Life: A Guidebook for Parents
Linda Dahl · $16.95 US · ISBN: 978-1-937612-85-6 · E-book: 978-1-937612-86-3

The Joey Song: A Mother's Story of Her Son's Addiction
Sandra Swenson · $15.95 US · ISBN: 978-1-937612-71-9
E-book: 978-1-937612-72-6

Out of the Woods: A Woman's Guide to Long-Term Recovery
Diane Cameron · $15.95 US · ISBN: 978-1-937612-47-4
E-book: 978-1-937612-48-1

May I Sit with You: A Simple Approach to Meditation
Tom Catton • $15.95 US • ISBN: 978-1-937612-83-2 • E-book: 978-1-937612-84-9

REFERENCE

Behavioral Addiction: Screening, Assessment, and Treatment
An-Pyng Sun, PhD; Larry Ashley, EdS; Lesley Dickson, MD · $18.95 US
ISBN: 978-1-936290-97-0 · E-book: 978-1-937612-05-4

When the Servant Becomes the Master: A Comprehensive Addiction Guide
for Those Who Suffer from the Disease, the Loved Ones Affected by It,
and the Professionals Who Assist Them
Jason Z W Powers, MD · $18.95 US · ISBN: 978-1-936290-73-4
E-book: 978-1-936290-86-4